THE BEST CALENDAR DESIGN + GRAPHICS

ROCKPORT PUBLISHERS
ROCKPORT, MASSACHUSETTS
DISTRIBUTED BY NORTH LIGHT BOOKS
CINCINNATI, OHIO

Designer: **PandaMonium Designs**
Art Director: **Laura P. Herrmann**
Cover Photographs: *Front Cover (left to right)*
Pg. 12
Pg. 45
Pg. 43
Back Cover (top to bottom)
Pg. 51
Pg. 57
Pg. 39
Pg. 14
Pg. 45

First published in the United States of America by:
Rockport Publishers, Inc.
146 Granite Street
Rockport, Massachusetts 01966-1299 USA
Telephone: (508) 546-9590
Fax: (508) 546-7141

Distributed to the book trade and art trade in the U.S. by:
North Light, an imprint of
F&W Publications
1507 Dana Avenue
Cincinnati, Ohio 45207
Telephone: (513) 531-2222

Other Distribution by:
Rockport Publishers, Inc.
Rockport, Massachusetts 01966-1299

1-56496-164-8

10 9 8 7 6 5 4 3 2 1

Manufactured in Singapore by Regent Production Services (S) Pte. Ltd.

T A B L E   O F   CONTENTS

ACKNOWLEDGEMENTS

The awards program and this book would not have been possible without the help of our sponsors.

We wish to thank:
Calendar Promotions of Washington, Iowa
Schumann Printers, Inc. of Bellwood, Illinois
Spiral of Illinois of Chicago, Illinois
Vijuk Equipment, Inc. of Elmhurst, Illinois
American Custom Publishing of Libertyville, Illinois

We also wish to thank our awards program panel of judges for their time, effort, and expertise derived from more than 100 years of combined experience:

Sherman Hardaway of Calendar Promotions
James D. Ratcliff of Calendar Promotions
Becky Rogers of Day Dream Publishing, Inc.
Bob McLuckie of MindsEye/McLuckie Design
James J. Murray of Schumann Printers, Inc.
Pat Schumann of Schumann Printers, Inc.
Bruce Kappele of Spiral of Illinois
Marcia Rigg of Tony Stone Images
Brad Hook of TypoGrafics, Inc.
Michael Tomic of Vijuk Equipment, Inc.
Robert Vijuk of Vijuk Equipment, Inc.

And lastly, we at the Calendar Marketing Association would like to thank our many hundreds of global contestants for making the 1995 National and World Calendar Awards a joy and a success.

INTRODUCTION

Since calendars, like clocks, are found everywhere, many people take them for granted. But study them closely, as we do, and you'll discover in the pages that follow all of the artistry, creativity, and imaginative use of technology that goes into this collection of the best and brightest calendar designs in the world today.

We formed the Calendar Marketing Association (CMA) as a trade association for the entire calendar industry, representing the interests of designers, marketers, publishers, printers, and suppliers of retail and custom calendars.

At the CMA we keep track of the latest trends and innovations in calendar publishing and marketing. We share that information with others in the field through CalendarNews, our official newsletter, and each year we present awards on a national and international level to calendar producers.

To celebrate the Calendar Marketing Association's fifth anniversary, we are proud to present this first annual volume of National and World Calendar Award winners.

Award winners were chosen from among hundreds of calendar submissions. All 1995 calendars produced in 1994 by any United States organization were eligible for entry in the National Calendar Awards, and all 1995 calendars produced in 1994 by any international organization were eligible for entry in the World Calendar Awards.

National calendar award winners are organized into four separate divisions: Advertising Specialty, Custom/Corporate, Retail, and Technical.

Advertising Specialty calendars are designed with a special area for imprinting or personalization. Custom/Corporate calendars are promotional calendars with an ongoing use specifically produced for a particular organization. Retail calendars are those purchased by consumers, or generally sold through stores and direct mail. The Technical division calendars are judged solely on technical merit within their entry category.

A panel of judges, representing the fields of design, photography, graphic arts, and calendar production, selected the winners in each category. Each judge scored calendars on a scale of one to one hundred. The judges' scores were then totaled and averaged for gold, silver, bronze, and merit awards in each category.

Sugar Hill Franconia, NH

jan.						
sun	mon	tues	wed	thurs	fri	sat
1	2	3	4	5	6	7
8	9	10	11	12	13	14
15	16	17	18	19	20	21
22	23	24	25		27	28
29	30					

feb.						
sun	mon	tues	wed	thurs	fri	sat
			1	2	3	4
5	6	7	8	9	10	11
12	13	14	15	16	17	18
19	20	21	22	23	24	25
26	27	28				

MARCH
S M T W T F S

Foremost Printers, Incorporated
1995

Take a photo of quaint, cobblestoned Acorn Street on Boston's historic Beacon Hill. Apply a unique blend of foil and ink so that the photo glimmers in three-dimensional glory. The result? The striking cover of Scenes of New England, the winner of the 1995 Rodney A. Andersen Best of Show award.

Like the cover, the pages that follow do not disappoint. Each photo in Scenes of New England, a wall calendar, submitted by Foremost Printers, Inc. of Stoughton, MA, offers a breath-taking view of what makes our northeastern states so special.

The calendar conveys the diversity of Foremost Printers, Inc., especially their electronic capabilities, specialized engraving, and RJM Graphics' patented prismatic imaging process.

Designer: Mike Gillette, Foremost Printers, Inc.

Engraver: David Larsen, Adolph Bauer, Inc.

ADDITIONAL AWARDS:
World & National GOLD—Best Finishing

1

B E S T
Classical Art

White Flower, 1932. Oil on panel, 26 x 20 inches (40.6 x 50.8 cm). Muscarelle Museum of Art, College of William and Mary in Virginia. Gift of Mrs. John D. Rockefeller, Jr.

June 1995

Sunday	Monday	Tuesday	Wednesday	Thursday	Friday	Saturday
				1	2	3
4	5	6	7	8	9	10
11	12	13	14	15	16	17
18	19	20	21	22	23	24
25	26	27	28	29	30	

Georgia O'Keeffe • One Hundred Flowers

Entered by: Callaway Editions, Inc.
National Award: **GOLD**
Class: Wall
Division: Retail

Beautiful Dreamers

Entered by: Portal Publications
National Award: GOLD
Class: Wall
Division: Retail
Designer & Art Director: Rebecca Hubert

Romance of the Past

Entered by: Graphique De France
World Award: SILVER
Class: Wall

French Impressionists

Entered by: Day Dream Publishing, Inc.
National Award: SILVER
Class: Miscellaneous
Division: Retail
Printer: Shepard Poorman
  Communications Corporation

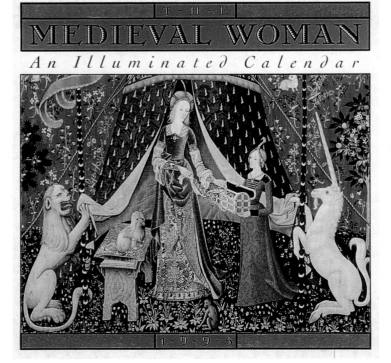

The Medieval Woman: An Illuminated Calendar for 1995 by Sally Fox

Entered by: Workman Publishing Company
World Award: SILVER
Class: Wall
Division: Retail
Text: Martha Driver

ADDITIONAL AWARD:
National MERIT—Best Classical Art

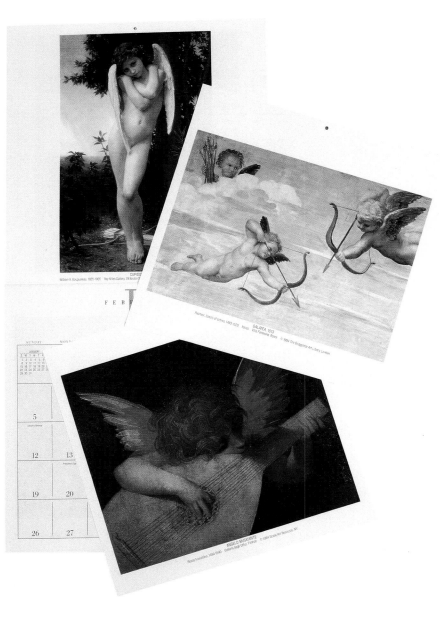

Angels
Entered by: Portal Publications
National Award: SILVER
Class: Wall
Division: Retail
Designer & Art Director: Sandra Belda

Georgia O'Keeffe
Entered by: Callaway Editions, Inc.
National Award: SILVER
Class: Desk
Division: Retail

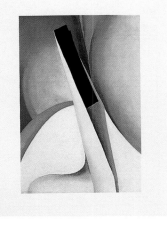

Timeline Two-Year Planner
Entered by: Keith Clark
National Award: BRONZE
Class: Pocket/Planner
Division: Retail

⭐

The Pre-Raphaelites
Entered by: Portal Publications
National Award: **BRONZE**
Class: Wall
Division: Retail
Designer & Art Director:
  Rebecca Hubert

⭐

Currier & Ives Petite
Entered by: JII/Sales Promotion
  Associates, Inc.
National Award: **BRONZE**
Class: Wall
Division: Advertising Specialty
Artist: Currier & Ives
Designer & Printer: JII/Sales
  Promotion Associates, Inc.

2

BEST

Contemporary Art

GOLD   SILVER   BRONZE   MERIT

Cochery-Bourdin-Chausse 1995
Entered by: d'OLCE
World Award: GOLD
Class: Wall
Designer: d'OLCE
Publisher: Cochery-Bourdin-Chausse

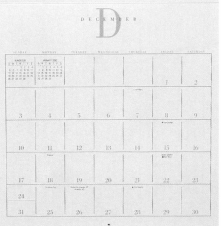

Images of Earth

Entered by: JII/Sales Promotion
 Associates, Inc.
National Award: **GOLD**
Class: Wall
Division: Advertising Specialty
Artist: Schim Schimmel
Designer & Printer: JII/Sales Promotion
 Associates, Inc.

ADDITIONAL AWARD:
World SILVER—Best Contemporary Art

Sea of Dreams by David Christopher Miller

Entered by: Portal Publications
National Award: **GOLD**
Class: Wall
Division: Retail
Designer: Raul Del Rio
Art Director: Rebecca Hubert

Underwater Fantasies

Entered by: Day Dream Publishing, Inc.
National Award: **GOLD**
Class: Miscellaneous
Division: Retail
Printer: Shepard Poorman
  Communications Corporation

The 1995 Best of Cleveland Calendar

Entered by: Modern International
  Graphics, Inc.
World Award: **GOLD**
Class: Wall
Division: Custom/Corporate

ADDITIONAL AWARD:
National GOLD—Best Contemporary Art

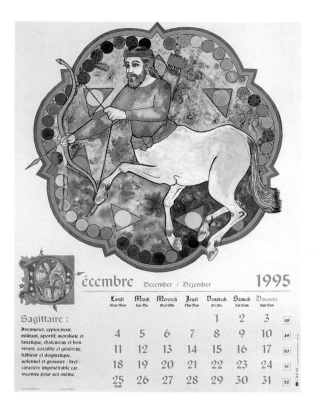

Zodiaque 1995
Entered by: KANTARO
World Award: SILVER
Class: Wall
Designer: KANTARO
Publisher: LAVIGNE

Chelsea Arts Club Yearbook
Entered by: Chelsea Ex-Centrics
National Award: SILVER
Class: Miscellaneous
Division: Custom/Corporate

ADDITIONAL AWARD:
World SILVER—Best Contemporary Art

Leonard Marchant *Autumn Table* 1990 oil

Abendakt 9.94 - 8.95

Entered by: Leissing Artgroup
World Award: SILVER
Class: Desk
Artwork: Leissing Artgroup
Designer & Art Director: Kurt Dornig
Printer: Carini Etiketten

Artists from the Art Academy of Cincinnati
Entered by: The C.J. Krehbiel Company
National Award: SILVER
Class: Wall
Division: Custom/Corporate

Carousel Magic
Entered by: Associated Advertising Agency
National Award: SILVER
Class: Poster
Division: Custom/Corporate
Client: Chance Rides, Inc.

Journey
Entered by: Tower Records
National Award: **SILVER**
Class: Poster
Division: Custom/Corporate
Artist: Gary Pruner
Designer & Art Director: Sharleen Lee
Printer: Fong & Fong Printers
 & Lithographers

**Jane Wooster Scott
Appointment Calendar**
Entered by: JII/Sales Promotion
 Associates, Inc.
National Award: **SILVER**
Class: Wall
Division: Advertising Specialty
Artist: Jane Wooster Scott
Designer & Printer: JII/Sales
 Promotion Associates, Inc.

The 1995 Lang Folk Art Calendar

Entered by: Lang Graphics, Ltd.
National Award: SILVER
Class: Wall
Division: Retail

The Art of Armand Frederick Vallée 1995 Desert Calendar

Entered by: Partners in Art U.S.A.
National Award: SILVER
Class: Desk
Division: Advertising Specialty
Designer: Ms. B.R. Vallée

ADDITIONAL AWARDS:
World SILVER—Best Contemporary Art
National GOLD—Best Graphic Design

1995 Butterflies

Entered by: Crane Creek Graphics
National Award: **BRONZE**
Class: Wall
Division: Retail

1995 Interim Health Care Calendar

Entered by: American Custom
  Publishing, Inc.
National Award: **BRONZE**
Class: Wall
Division: Advertising Specialty
Art Director: Patricia Henze

Friends & Relatives:
The 1995 Calendar
by Fred Babb
Entered by: Workman Publishing Company
World Award: BRONZE
Class: Wall

**Epi Schlüsselberger
Schrift-Bilder**

Entered by: Epi Schlüsselberger
World Award: **BRONZE**
Class: Wall
Designer: Epi Schlüsselberger
Printer: UngarDruck
Reproduction: Repro12

Timeline Two-Year Planner

Entered by: Keith Clark
National Award: BRONZE
Class: Pocket/Planner
Division: Retail

Pittsburgh Illustrated 1995 Calendar

Entered by: Susan Castriota,
 Greetings from Pittsburgh
National Award: MERIT
Class: Wall
Division: Advertising Specialty
Designer & Illustrator: Susan Castriota

The Heritage Foundation 1995 Oswego County Landmark Calendar

Entered by: Oswego County Boces
National Award: MERIT
Class: Wall
Division: Custom/Corporate
Designers & Illustrators:
 Commercial Art Students

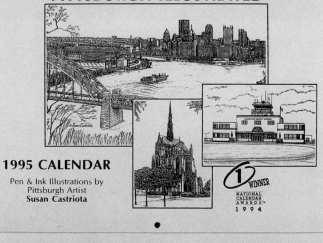

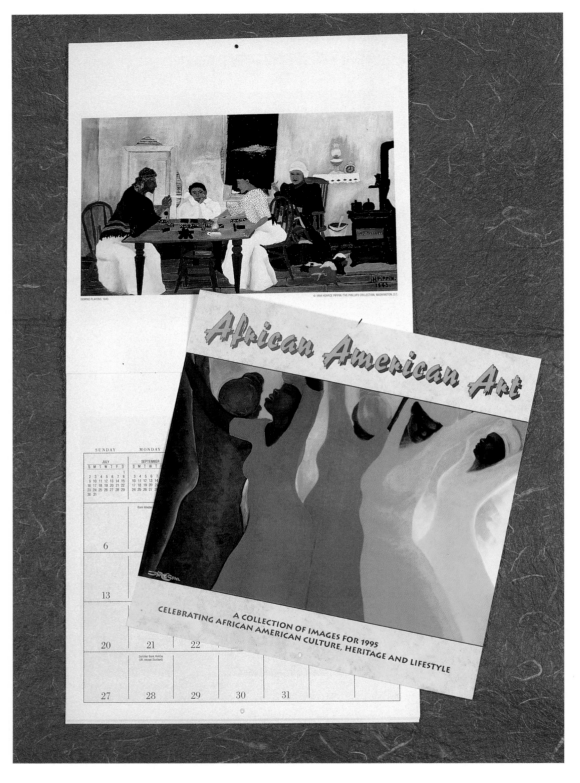

African American Art
Entered by: Portal Publications
National Award: MERIT
Class: Wall
Division: Retail
Designer: Raul Del Rio
Art Director: Jennifer Reno

3

B E S T
Production

Color Separation

Finishing

Printing

Use of Paper

GOLD   SILVER   BRONZE   MERIT

**French Country Diary 1995
by Pierre Moulin, Pierre
Le Vec, and Linda Dannenberg**
Entered by: Workman Publishing Company
National Award: SILVER
Class: Desk
Division: Technical
Photographer: Guy Bonchet

**John Grossman's Victorian
Charms 1995 Pocket Planner**
Entered by: Shepard Poorman
 Communications Corporation
National Award: SILVER
Class: Pocket/Planner
Division: Technical
Publisher: Day Dream Publishing, Inc.

COLOR SEPARATION

MANGELSEN

Images Of Nature®
1995 CALENDAR

Mangelsen/Images Of Nature
Entered by: Images Of Nature
National Award: **BRONZE**
Class: Wall
Division: Technical, Retail
Designer: Tom Debuse, Lortz Direct
   Marketing Inc.

ADDITIONAL AWARD:
National SILVER—Best Nature/
   Scenic Photography

Romancing the Eye

Entered by: Progress Printing
National Award: MERIT
Class: Wall
Divisions: Technical, Custom/Corporate
Designer: Joy Satterwhite
Photographer: Al Satterwhite
Prepress & Printing: Progress Printing

ADDITIONAL AWARDS:
World MERIT—Best Printing
National SILVER—Best Finishing
National BRONZE—Best Use of Paper
National MERIT—Most Original

1995 Superior Premier Graphics Calendar

Entered by: Superior Premier Graphics
National Award: BRONZE
Class: Poster
Division: Technical

Victorian Treasures

Entered by: Hallmark Cards, Inc.
National Award: MERIT
Class: Wall
Division: Technical
Designer: Calendar Design Group
Printer: Commercial Lithographers
Client: Hallmark Cards, Inc.

Tempus Organizer

Entered by: Tempus Germany
World Award: SILVER
Class: Desk

FINISHING

JANUARY | JANVIER | JANUAR

Paul
GAUGUIN

1995
Calendar

Scenes of New England

Entered by: Foremost Printers, Inc.
World Award: GOLD
Class: Wall
Division: Technical

ADDITIONAL AWARDS:
National BEST OF SHOW AWARD
 (see page 6)
National GOLD—Best Finishing

Paul Gauguin

Entered by: Graphique De France
World Award: BRONZE
Class: Wall

PRINTING

Yosemite - Photographs by William Neill

Entered by: Dumont Printing

National Award: GOLD

Class: Wall

Division: Technical

Designer & Art Director:
Kristi Carlson

Printer: Dumont Printing

ADDITIONAL AWARDS:

World, National GOLD—
Best Color Separation

World GOLD, National BRONZE—
Best Graphic Design

World SILVER, National GOLD—
Best Typography

World BRONZE—Best Printing,
Most Original, Best Nature/
Scenic Photography

Images '95
Entered by: Spiral of Illinois, Inc.
World Award: **GOLD**
Class: Wall
Division: Technical
Designers: Robert D. Fink and
William Rousos, Superior
Colour Graphics
Printer: Superior Colour Graphics

ADDITIONAL AWARD:
National SILVER—Best Printing

Henri Matisse
Entered by: Graphique De France
World Award: **SILVER**
Class: Desk

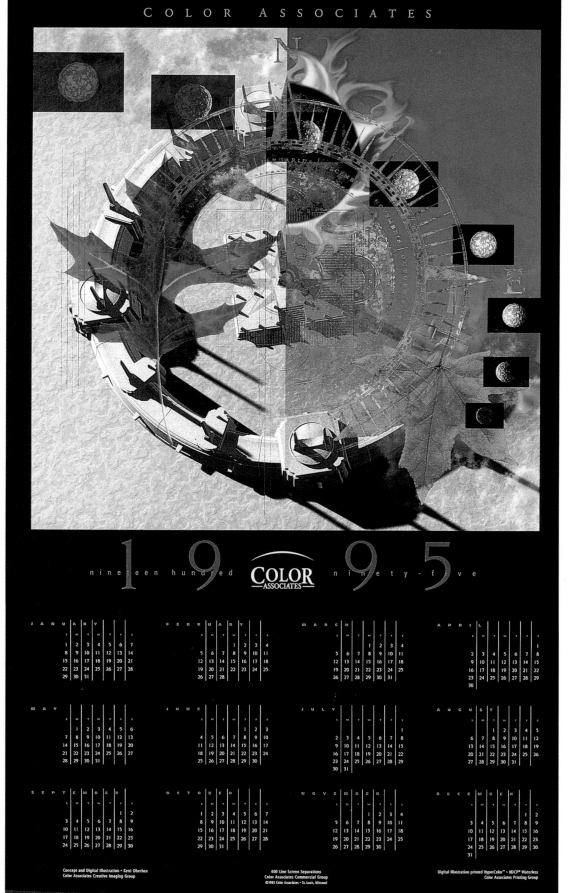

Color Associates 1995 Promotional Calendar

Entered by: Color Associates
National Award: SILVER
Class: Poster
Divisions: Technical,
 Custom/Corporate

ADDITIONAL AWARDS:
World SILVER—Best Printing
National SILVER—Best
 Contemporary Art

S&S Graphics
1995 Calendar

Entered by: S&S Graphics, Inc.
National Award: SILVER
Class: Poster
Divisions: Technical, Custom/Corporate
Designer: S&S Graphics, Inc.

ADDITIONAL AWARDS:
World SILVER—Best Printing,
 Best Classical Art
National SILVER—Best Classical Art

Images 1995

Entered by: Stephenson Printing
National Award: SILVER
Class: Wall
Divisions: Technical,
 Custom/Corporate
Art Director: George E. Stephenson

ADDITIONAL AWARDS:
World, National SILVER—
 Best Classical Art
World SILVER—Best Printing

Lake County Press - 25 Years
Entered by: Lake County Press, Inc.
National Award: **BRONZE**
Class: Wall
Divisions: Technical, Custom/Corporate

ADDITIONAL AWARDS:
National BRONZE—
 Best Graphic Design, Best Finishing
National MERIT—
 Best Nature/Scenic Photography,
 Best Color Separation

**The 365 Cars Page-A-Day®
Full-Color Calendar**
Entered by: Workman
 Publishing Company
National Award: **SILVER**
Class: Desk
Division: Technical

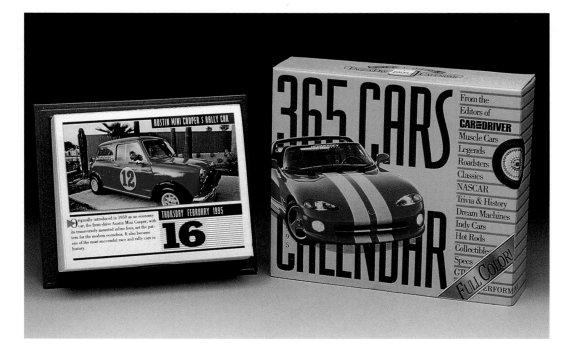

Every Day is a New Year's Day
Entered by:
 Fischbachpresse/Fischwerkstatt
World Award: SILVER
Class: Wall

USE OF
PAPER

JULI

MONTAG	DIENSTAG	MITTWOCH	DONNERSTAG	FREITAG	SAMSTAG	SONNTAG
					1	2
3	4	5	6	7	8	9
10	11	12	13	14	15	16
17	18	19	20	21	22	23
24	25	26	27	28	29	30
31						

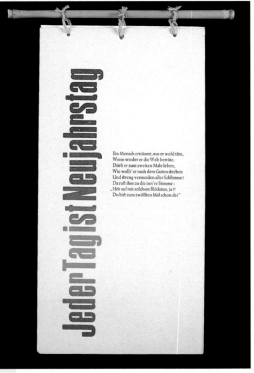

Workbook Calendar 1995

Entered by: The Workbook
National Award: SILVER
Class: Desk
Division: Technical

Tempus Organizer

Entered by: Tempus Germany
World Award: SILVER
Class: Pocket/Planner

ADDITIONAL AWARDS:
World SILVER—Best Typography,
Best Printing, Most Original

**William Adolphe
Bouguereau**
Entered by: Graphique De France
World Award: SILVER
Class: Wall

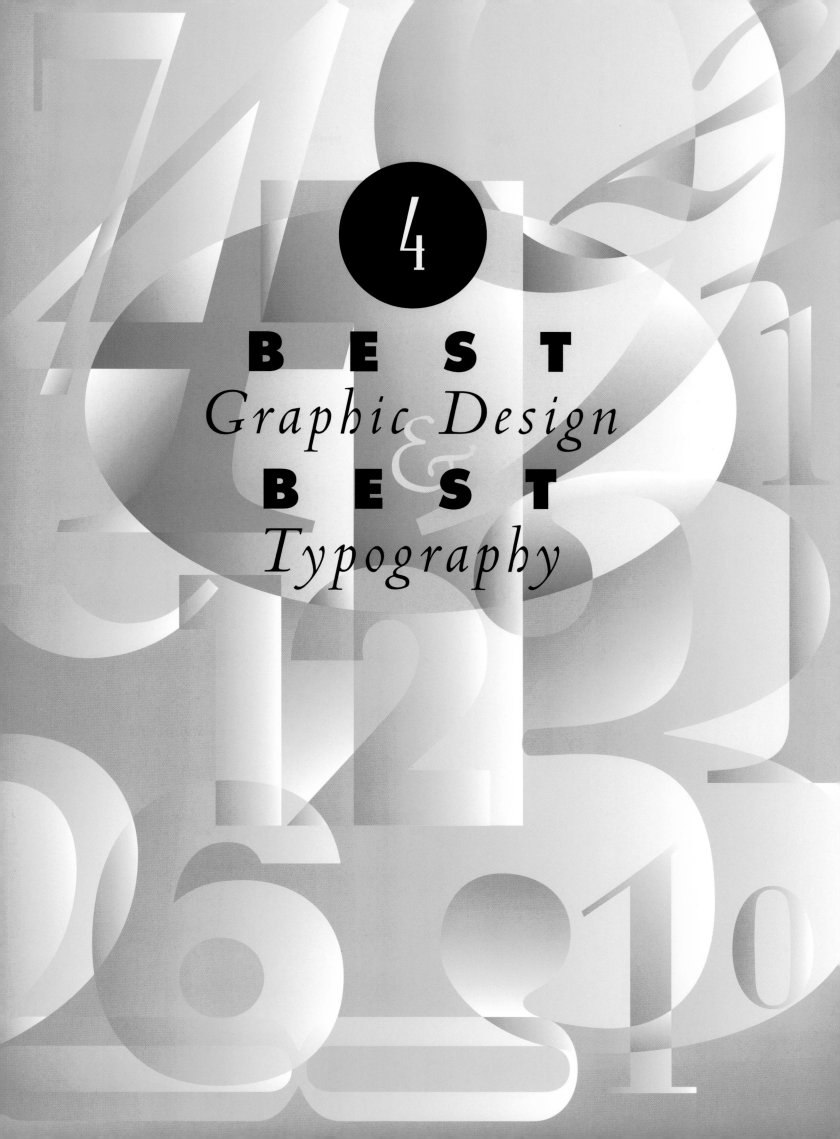

4

BEST
Graphic Design
& BEST
Typography

GOLD SILVER BRONZE MERIT

GRAPHIC
DESIGN

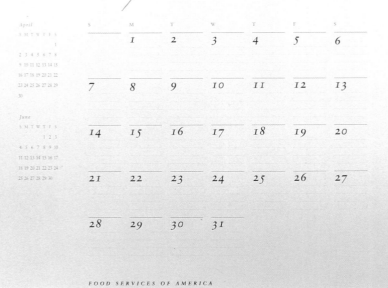

Food Services of America
1995 Calendar

Entered by: Hornall Anderson Design Works

National Award: **GOLD**

Class: Wall

Division: Custom/Corporate

Designers: Jack Anderson,
 Mary Hermes, and Julie Keenan

Calligrapher: Georgia Deaver

Art Director: Jack Anderson

Photographer: Tom Collicot

ADDITIONAL AWARD:

World BRONZE—Best Graphic Design

Curiosities of the Season 1995

Entered by: Leslie Evans Design

National Award: GOLD

Class: Wall

Division: Technical

Designers: Leslie Evans and Mary Brown

Creative Director: Leslie Evans

Photographers: Susie Cushner, Carl Hyatt, and Sara Gray

Stylist: Barbara Kurgan

Printer: Penmor Lithographers

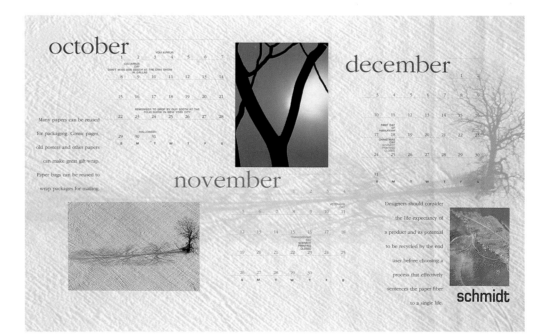

Schmidt Printing Calendar

Entered by: MC Studio/Times Mirror Magazines

National Award: GOLD

Class: Poster

Division: Custom/Corporate

Designer: Monica Götz

Art Director: Paul Kelly

Consolite Corporation Calendar

Entered by: Tracy Sabin Graphic Design
National Award: **GOLD**
Class: Poster
Division: Custom/Corporate
Illustrator: Tracy Sabin
Art Director: Robert Stetzel
Printer: Consolite Corporation

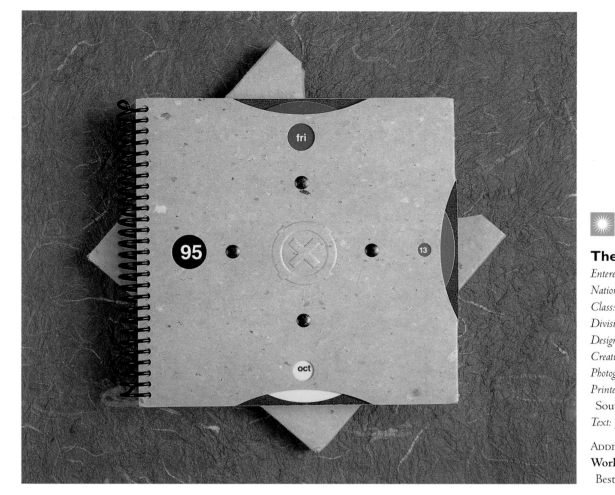

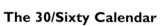

The 30/Sixty Calendar

Entered by: 30/Sixty design inc.
National Award: **GOLD**
Class: Desk
Division: Custom/Corporate
Designer: Pär Larsson
Creative Director: Henry Vizcarra
Photographer: Scott Hensel
Printer: Digital Imaging of
  Southern California
Text: J.C. Bennett

ADDITIONAL AWARD:
World BRONZE—
 Best Graphic Design

Pro Planner 2-Pages Per Day Complete Planning Kit

Entered by: Day Runner, Inc.
World Award: **GOLD**
Class: Pocket/Planner

Dalmation 1994-1995 Student Planner

Entered by: Landmark General Corp.

National Award: **GOLD**

Class: Pocket/Planner

Division: Retail

Eighteen Month Planner

Entered by: Pletka Design

National Award: **GOLD**

Class: Pocket/Planner

Division: Custom/Corporate

Designer: Diane Pletka

Illustrator: Bohn Illustration

Photographer: Bakstad Photographics

Printer: Luxon Printing

Expressive Images-
Golf Planner
Entered by: Keith Clark
National Award: **GOLD**
Class: Pocket/Planner
Division: Retail

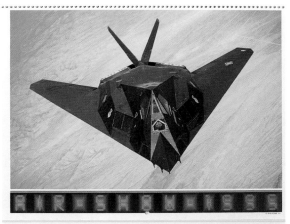

Air Show
Entered by: JII/Sales Promotion
  Associates, Inc.
National Award: **GOLD**
Class: Wall
Division: Advertising Specialty
Designer & Printer: JII/Sales
  Promotion Associates, Inc.

Tempus Organizer
Entered by: Tempus Germany
World Award: GOLD
Class: Desk

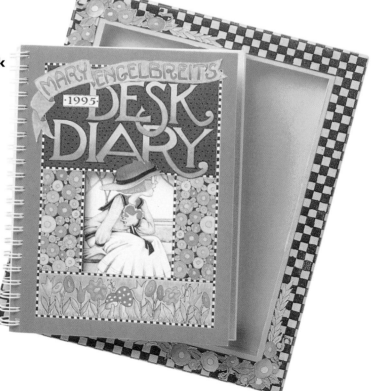

Mary Engelbreit's Desk Diary 1995
Entered by: Workman Publishing Company
National Award: GOLD
Class: Desk
Division: Retail

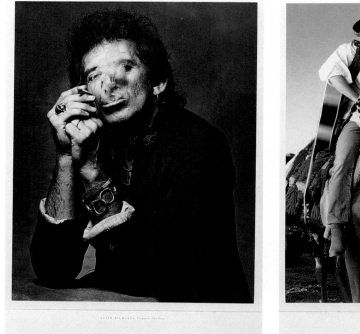

MARCH
1 9 9 5

Sunday	Monday	Tuesday	Wednesday	Thursday	Friday	Saturday
			1	2	3	4
5	6	7	8	9	10	11
12	13	14	15	16	17	18
19	20	21	22	23	24	25
26	27	28	29	30	31	

DECEMBER
1 9 9 5

Sunday	Monday	Tuesday	Wednesday	Thursday	Friday	Saturday
					1	2
3	4	5	6	7	8	9
10	11	12	13	14	15	16
17	18	19	20	21	22	23
24 31	25	26	27	28	29	30

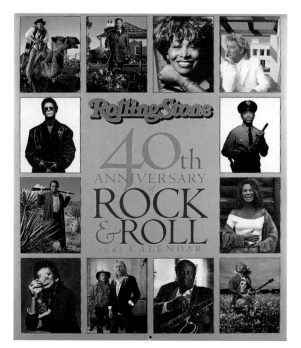

**Rolling Stone
40th Anniversary
Rock and Roll Calendar**
Entered by: Callaway Editions, Inc.
National Award: **GOLD**
Class: Wall
Division: Retail

TIAA-CREF 1995 Staff
Benefits Planning Diary

Entered by: Paganucci Design, Inc.
National Award: SILVER
Class: Pocket/Planner
Division: Custom/Corporate
Designers: Frank Paganucci
  and Rafael Sanchez
Creative Director: Bob Paganucci

**1995 Enteron
Desktop Calendar**

Entered by: Enteron Group
National Award: SILVER
Class: Desk
Division: Technical

Timeframe™ Calendar

Entered by: Designframe Incorporated
National Award: SILVER
Class: Desk
Division: Advertising Specialty
Designer & Art Director: James A. Sebastian

My Secret Gardens

Entered by: Hammond's, Inc.
National Award: MERIT
Class: Wall
Division: Retail
Designer: Dunn-Allen Design and
  Colorations, Inc.
Printer: International Graphics, Inc.

Guess?, Inc. 1995 Agenda

Entered by: Guess?, Inc.
National Award: SILVER
Class: Pocket/Planner
Division: Custom/Corporate
Designer: Leslie Oki
Art Director: Paul Marciano
Printer: Southern California Graphics

Earth in Focus

Entered by: American Airlines
 Magazine Publications
National Award: SILVER
Class: Wall
Division: Custom/Corporate
Designers: Kyle Dreier
 and Scott Feaster
Printer: ColorMark

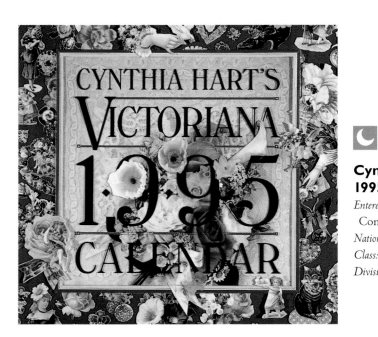

**Cynthia Hart's Victoriana
1995 Calendar**

Entered by: Workman Publishing
 Company
National Award: SILVER
Class: Wall
Division: Retail

**At-A-Glance Brand
800 Range**
Entered by: Keith Clark
National Award: SILVER
Class: Pocket/Planner
Division: Retail

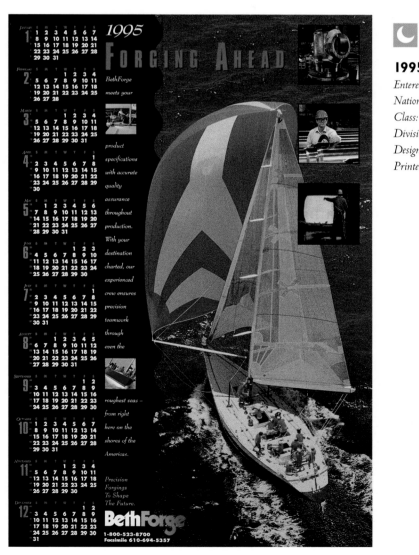

1995 Forging Ahead
Entered by: Lieberman-Appalucci
National Award: SILVER
Class: Poster
Division: Custom/Corporate
Designer: Debbie Martin
Printer: Phototype

Thomas Kinkade Painter of Light™ 1995 Engagement Diary

Entered by: AMCAL
World Award: SILVER
Class: Desk

Pocket Planner Tapestry

Entered by: Day Runner, Inc.
World Award: SILVER
Class: Pocket/Planner

Elements of Time

Entered by: Designframe
  Incorporated
National Award: SILVER
Class: Desk
Division: Custom/Corporate
Designers: James A. Sebastian
  and Frank Nichols
Art Director: Michael McGinn
Creative Director: James A. Sebastian
Printer: Diversified Graphics
  Incorporated
Typographer: James Lung

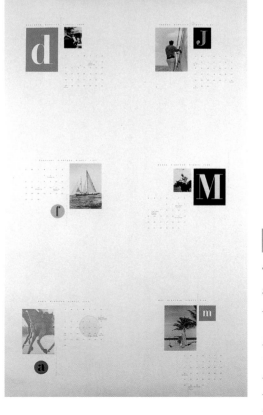

Dream Fields

Entered by: Chronicle Books

National Award: SILVER

Class: Desk

Division: Retail

Designer: Sarah Bolles

Photographer: Jim Dow

**Town Center
at Boca Raton**

Entered by:
  Hershey Communications, Inc.

National Award: SILVER

Class: Poster

Division: Custom/Corporate

Designer: Mario Avila

Printer: Colombia Lithograph

Color Separator: Adventures

Sawmill Days

Entered by: Dusseau Design
National Award: SILVER
Class: Pocket/Planner
Division: Technical
Designer: Terri S. Dusseau
Printer: Fine Line Graphics

4-1-1 Student Planner

Entered by: Day Runner, Inc.
National Award: **SILVER**
Class: Pocket/Planner
Division: Retail

Corey & Company: Designers '95 National Calendar

Entered by: Corey & Company: Designers
National Award: **SILVER**
Class: Pocket/Planner
Division: Technical
Designers: Susan Gilzow
  and Tammy Radmer
Printer: Reynolds-DeWalt Printing

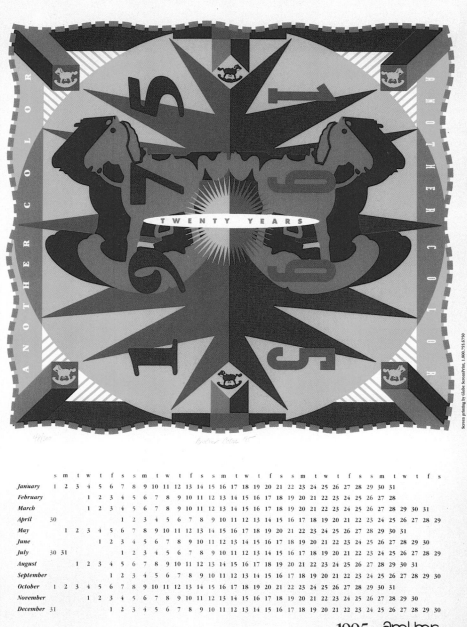

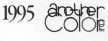

	s	m	t	w	t	f	s	s	m	t	w	t	f	s	s	m	t	w	t	f	s	s	m	t	w	t	f	s	s	m	t	w	t	f	s
January	1	2	3	4	5	6	7	8	9	10	11	12	13	14	15	16	17	18	19	20	21	22	23	24	25	26	27	28	29	30	31				
February			1	2	3	4	5	6	7	8	9	10	11	12	13	14	15	16	17	18	19	20	21	22	23	24	25	26	27	28					
March			1	2	3	4	5	6	7	8	9	10	11	12	13	14	15	16	17	18	19	20	21	22	23	24	25	26	27	28	29	30	31		
April	30						1	2	3	4	5	6	7	8	9	10	11	12	13	14	15	16	17	18	19	20	21	22	23	24	25	26	27	28	29
May		1	2	3	4	5	6	7	8	9	10	11	12	13	14	15	16	17	18	19	20	21	22	23	24	25	26	27	28	29	30	31			
June					1	2	3	4	5	6	7	8	9	10	11	12	13	14	15	16	17	18	19	20	21	22	23	24	25	26	27	28	29	30	
July	30	31					1	2	3	4	5	6	7	8	9	10	11	12	13	14	15	16	17	18	19	20	21	22	23	24	25	26	27	28	29
August		1	2	3	4	5	6	7	8	9	10	11	12	13	14	15	16	17	18	19	20	21	22	23	24	25	26	27	28	29	30	31			
September				1	2	3	4	5	6	7	8	9	10	11	12	13	14	15	16	17	18	19	20	21	22	23	24	25	26	27	28	29	30		
October	1	2	3	4	5	6	7	8	9	10	11	12	13	14	15	16	17	18	19	20	21	22	23	24	25	26	27	28	29	30	31				
November			1	2	3	4	5	6	7	8	9	10	11	12	13	14	15	16	17	18	19	20	21	22	23	24	25	26	27	28	29	30			
December	31			1	2	3	4	5	6	7	8	9	10	11	12	13	14	15	16	17	18	19	20	21	22	23	24	25	26	27	28	29	30		

Twenty Years
Entered by: Another Color Inc.
World Award: SILVER
Class: Poster
Art Director: Sam Halton
Printer: Globe Screenprint

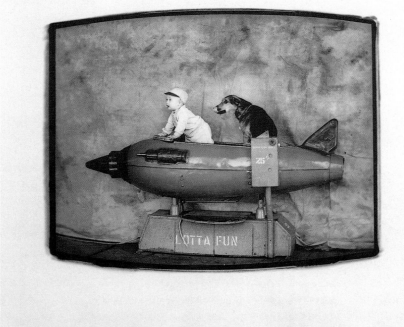

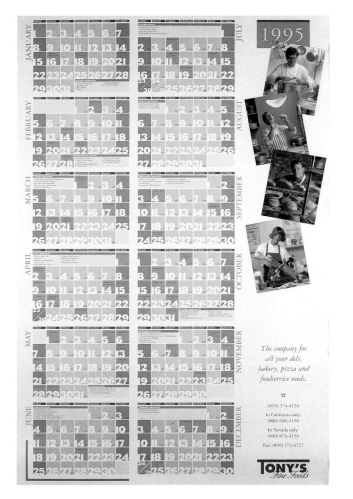

Good Dog! 1995 Calendar
Entered by: Chronicle Books
National Award: **BRONZE**
Class: Wall
Division: Retail
Designer: Madeleine Carson Design
Photographer: Robyn Stoutenberg,
   courtesy of Swanstock Agency

Tony's
Entered by: Marketing by Design
National Award: **BRONZE**
Class: Poster
Division: Custom/Corporate
Designer: Joel Stinghen
Photographer: Kent Lacin
Printer: Graphic Center

State of the Art

Entered by: The John Roberts Co.
National Award: **BRONZE**
Class: Desk
Division: Custom/Corporate
Designer: Randy Larson

Blenheim Trade Show 1995 Planner

Entered by: Eleanor Wong Designs
National Award: **BRONZE**
Class: Poster
Division: Custom/Corporate
Designers: Helene Bramming and
 Deborah Van Walsum
Art Director: Eleanor S. Wong
Client: Blenheim Group U.S.A., Inc.

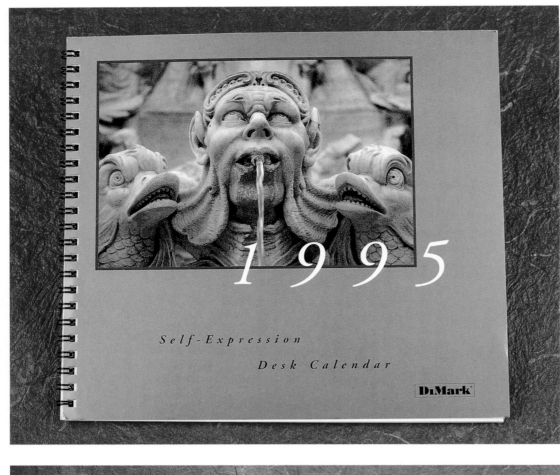

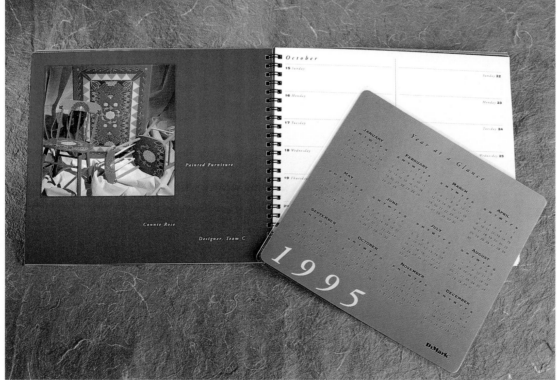

**Self-Expression
Desk Calendar**
Entered by: DiMark, Inc.
National Award: MERIT
Class: Desk
Division: Custom/Corporate
Designer: Anita Gagliardi
Printer: Baum Printing
Text: Gregg Oliver

A Year in Flowers

Entered by: Chronicle Books
National Award: MERIT
Class: Desk
Division: Retail
Designer: Lucille Tenazas Design
Photographer: Debra Heimerdinger

1995 Traffic Calendar

Entered by:
 Traffic Advertising & Printing
National Award: MERIT
Class: Desk
Division: Custom/Corporate

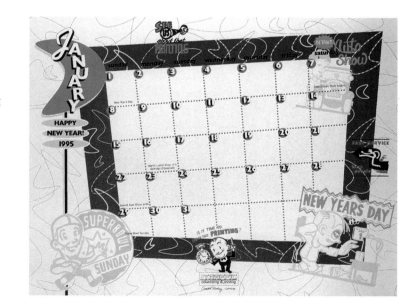

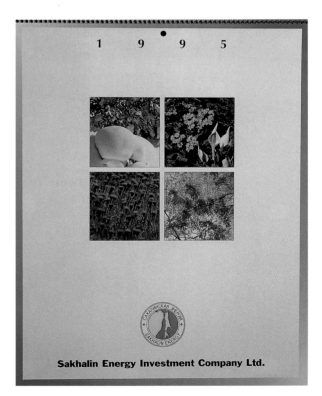

A Celebration
of Classic Toys

Entered by: Federated Investors
National Award: MERIT
Class: Wall
Division: Custom/Corporate
Designer: Richard A. Sciullo
Production Specialist: Lauren Prescott
Text: Kristin Dillon

Sakhalin Energy Calendar

Entered by: Marathon Oil Company
World Award: MERIT
Class: Wall
Designer: Sandy Mathios
Production: Marathon Graphics

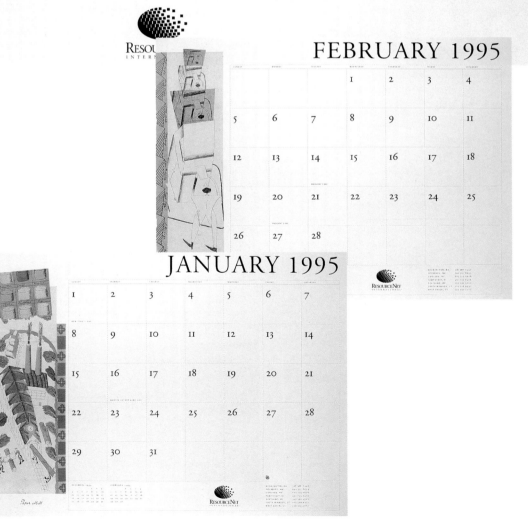

**1995 ResourceNet
International**
Entered by: DeFrancis Studio
National Award: MERIT
Class: Desk
Division: Custom/Corporate
Illustrator: Philipe Weisbecker
Art Director: Greg Galvan

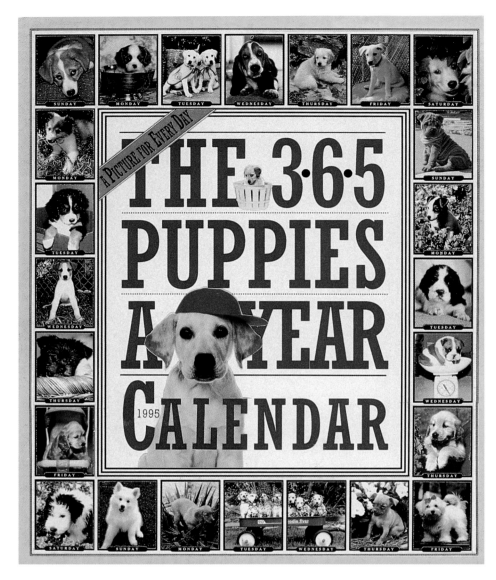

The 365 Puppies-A-Year Calendar for 1995

Entered by: Workman Publishing Company
National Award: MERIT
Class: Wall
Division: Retail

World Port of Duluth

Entered by: Westmoreland Larson Webster Inc.
World Award: SILVER
Class: Poster
Division: Custom/Corporate
Designer: Steve Isola
Printer: P.G.I.

ADDITIONAL AWARD:
National MERIT—
Best Graphic Design

TYPOGRAPHY

The Pink Panther
Entered by: Graphique De France
World Award: SILVER
Class: Wall

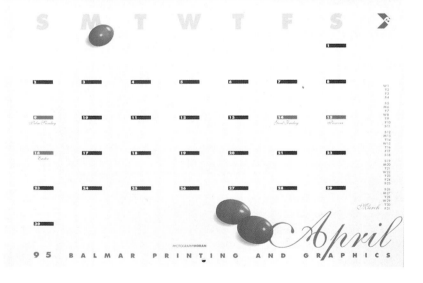

Change

Entered by: Balmar Printing
   & Graphics
National Award: **SILVER**
Class: Wall
Division: Technical
Designer: Renee Ramos
Art Director: Glenn Heitz

ADDITIONAL AWARDS:
National MERIT—Best Color
   Separation, Best Graphic Design

5

BEST

Photography

GLAMOUR

NATURE/SCENIC

GOLD   SILVER   BRONZE   MERIT

Guess? 1995 Calendar

Entered by: Guess?, Inc.

National Award: GOLD

Class: Wall

Division: Custom/Corporate

Designer: Leslie Oki

Art Director: Paul Marciano

Printer: Southern California Graphics

GLAMOUR

Miss Napa

Entered by: Calendar Promotions

National Award: SILVER

Class: Wall

Division: Custom/Corporate

**Men...RUNDU STYLE-
"The Heated Version"**
Entered by: Rundu Staggers
National Award: GOLD
Class: Wall
Division: Retail

**Remy's Swimsuit
Calendar 1995**
Entered by: Lehner International
World Award: SILVER
Class: Wall
Division: Retail
Designers: Remy and Daniel Lehner
Photographer: Ruth Eich
Printer: Castlereagh Press Inc.

ADDITIONAL AWARD:
National BRONZE—
 Best Glamour Photography

C A L E N D A R   1 9 9 5

BREAKING BOUNDS

THE DANCE PHOTOGRA...
LOIS GREENF...

NOVEMBER

Breaking Bounds
Entered by: Chronicle Books
National Award: SILVER
Class: Wall
Division: Retail
Designer: L. Creighton Dinsmore
 Design
Photographer: Lois Greenfield

1995 CALENDAR BRONZE BEAUTY

PHOTOGRAPHED BY HOWARD MOREHEAD

Bronze Beauty
Entered by: Bronze Beauty Enterprises
World Award: BRONZE
Class: Wall

★

**Dance Magazine Greetings
1995 Calendar**

Entered by: Dance Magazine
National Award: BRONZE
Class: Wall
Division: Custom/Corporate
Designer & Photographer: Herbert
 Migdoll
Printer: Prism Color Corporation

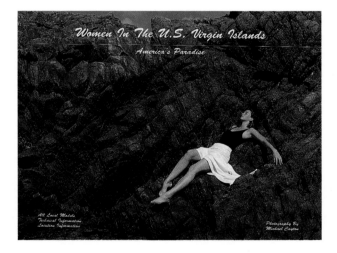

the Kiss

Entered by: Portal Publications
National Award: SILVER
Class: Wall
Division: Retail
Designer: Sandra Belda
Art Director: Jennifer Reno

𝔐

**Women in the U.S.
Virgin Islands**

Entered by: Photography by Michael
National Award: MERIT
Class: Wall
Division: Retail
Designer: L. Michael Cayton
Printer: Graphic Labs

National Geographic:
The Photographs

Entered by:
  National Geographic Society
National Award: GOLD
Class: Desk
Division: Retail

ADDITIONAL AWARD:
  World GOLD—Most Original

The World of Flight

Entered by: Sharon Ramey &
   Associates
National Award: **GOLD**
Class: Wall
Division: Advertising Specialty
Distributor: Sharon Ramey &
   Associates
Printer: Castle-Pierce
Publisher: Experimental Aircraft
   Association

**1995 Artist Feature
Calendar**

Entered by: Tom Hopkins Studio
National Award: **GOLD**
Class: Wall
Division: Custom/Corporate
Printer: Magnani & McCormick, Inc.

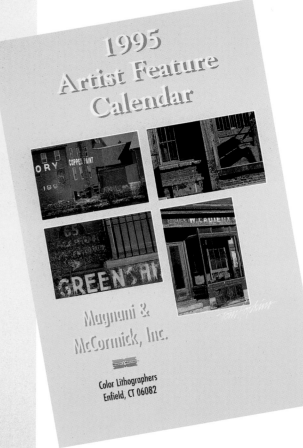

The Natural Moment
Entered by: Simon & Schuster
National Award: **GOLD**
Class: Wall
Division: Retail

JANUARY
MONDAY
23

TUESDAY ▶ last quarter
24

WEDNESDAY
25

THURSDAY
26

FRIDAY
27

SATURDAY/SUNDAY
28/29

Pristine wilderness.

Alaska is home to a diverse array of wildlife, including gray wolves, caribou, grizzlies, and Dall sheep.

JUNE
MONDAY
12

TUESDAY ○ full moon
13

WEDNESDAY
14

THURSDAY
15

FRIDAY
16

SATURDAY/SUNDAY Father's Day (Sunday)
17/18

The Rainbow Warrior crew finds a victim of a North Pacific driftnet.

Every year about 750,000 seabirds, ... Alaskan horned puffins, are ensnared by driftnets despite a U.N. moratorium.

Seasons
Entered by: Teldon Calendars
National Award: **SILVER**
Class: Wall
Division: Advertising Specialty
Designer & Printer: Teldon Calendars

Greenpeace Diary 1995
Entered by:
  Workman Publishing Company
World Award: **GOLD**
Class: Desk

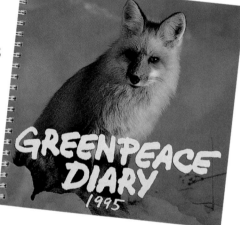

1995 Calendar

Entered by: Yamamoto Moss
National Award: SILVER
Class: Desk
Division: Custom/Corporate
Designers: Hideki Yamamoto and
  Brian Adducci
Client: Northwest Airlines

ADDITIONAL AWARDS:
World BRONZE—Best Nature/
  Scenic Photography
World MERIT—Most Original
National BRONZE—Most Original

Kennan Ward

Entered by: Kennan Ward
  Photography
National Award: SILVER
Class: Desk
Division: Retail
Printer: Hatcher Trade Press

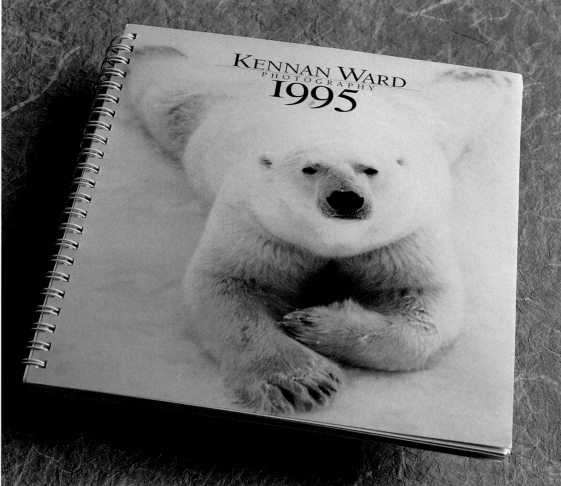

Talbot
Entered by:
  Graphique De France
World Award: **SILVER**
Class: Wall

Wildlife
Entered by: Teldon Calendars
National Award: **SILVER**
Class: Wall
Division: Advertising Specialty
Designer & Printer: Teldon Calendars

82

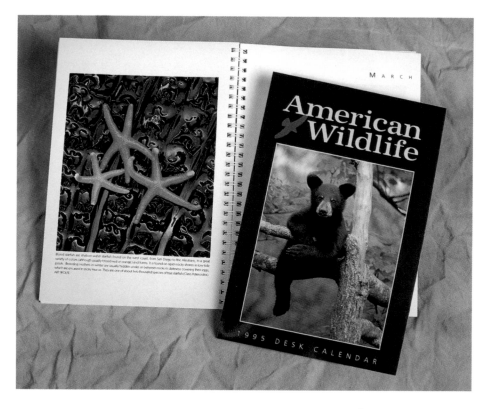

1995 American Wildlife Desk Calendar

Entered by: Falcon Press Publishing
National Award: BRONZE
Class: Desk
Division: Retail

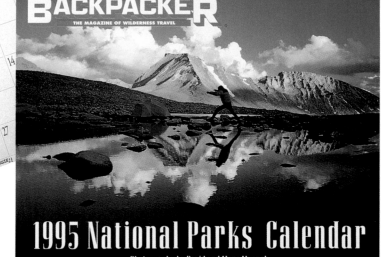

Backpacker 1995 National Parks Calendar

Entered by: Backpacker/Rodale Press
National Award: BRONZE
Class: Wall
Division: Retail
Designer & Art Director: John Pepper
Photo Editor: Deborah Burnett Stauffer
Photographers: David and Marc Muench
Text: Larry Rice

Midland Calendar

Entered by: LSY Advertising, Inc.
National Award: **MERIT**
Class: Wall
Division: Custom/Corporate
Photographer: Gregory Thorp
Printer: Hammer Graphics

Timeline Two-Year Planner

Entered by: Keith Clark
National Award: **MERIT**
Class: Pocket/Planner
Division: Retail

Executive Office

Entered by: JII/Sales Promotion
  Associates, Inc.
National Award: **BRONZE**
Class: Wall
Division: Advertising Specialty
Designer & Printer: JII/Sales
  Promotion Associates, Inc.

Sail 1995 Calendar

Entered by: Sail Magazine
National Award: MERIT
Class: Wall
Division: Retail
Printer: Bradley

**The Greenpeace
Calendar for 1995:
Stepping Lightly
on the Earth**
Entered by: Workman Publishing Company
World Award: MERIT
Class: Wall

6

MOST

Original

GOLD   SILVER   BRONZE   MERIT

Exceptional Views 1995

Entered by: Roadway Express, Inc.
National Award: **GOLD**
Class: Wall
Division: Custom/Corporate

ADDITIONAL AWARD:
National BRONZE—Most Creative
  Marketing Application

Wallner

Entered by: Arge Koschak, Widauer
World Award: **GOLD**
Class: Miscellaneous
Design & Text: Koschak & Widauer

The Artful Letter

Entered by: Marcy Robinson
National Award: **SILVER**
Class: Desk
Division: Retail
Cover Design: Marcy Robinson
Editors: Carole Maurer
 and Eleanor Winters
Publisher: Universe Publishing

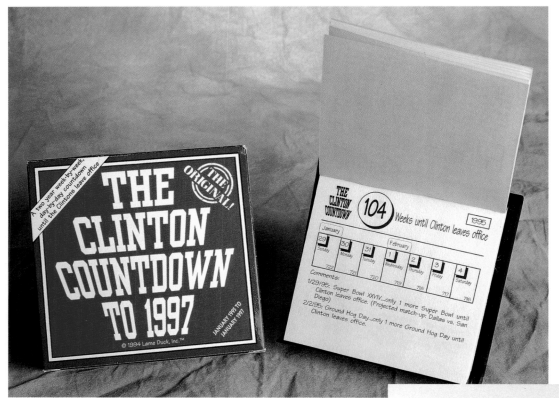

The Clinton Countdown to 1997: The Final Year

Entered by: Lame Duck, Inc.
National Award: SILVER
Class: Desk
Division: Retail

ADDITIONAL AWARD:
World MERIT—Most Original

Expresso™ Calendar & Address Book

Entered by: Berkeley Systems, Inc.
National Award: SILVER
Class: Miscellaneous
Division: Retail
Designer: Allard Laban

**A Year and A Day
Engagement Calendar**
Entered by: The Overlook Press
National Award: SILVER
Class: Pocket/Planner
Division: Retail

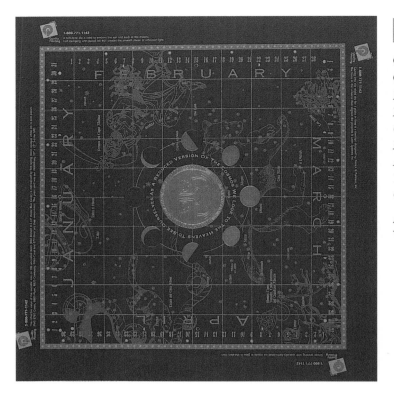

Quarterly Celestial Calendar

Entered by: Patrick & Partners, Inc.

National Award: SILVER

Class: Poster

Division: Custom/Corporate

Art Director: Mark Manuszak

Text: Alan Schoff

Client: Quality Printing

ADDITIONAL AWARD:

World MERIT—Best Theme

The Dog Portraits: A Calendar for 1995 by Thierry Poncelet

Entered by:
Workman Publishing Company

World Award: SILVER

Class: Wall

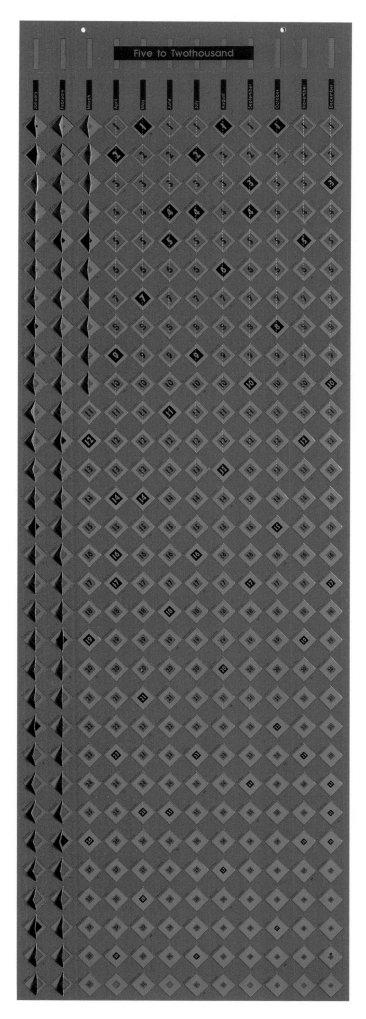

Edition 1995

Entered by: D & A Diego Bally AG
 Design & Advertising
World Award: **SILVER**
Class: Poster
Designer: Diego Bally

MoonShine 1995

Entered by: Celestial Products, Inc.
 and White Crescent Press, Ltd.
National Award: **SILVER**
Class: Poster
Divisions: Advertising Specialty, Retail
Designer: Larry Bohlayer

ADDITIONAL AWARDS:
World SILVER—Best Printing
National SILVER—Most Original

How To Be Bald?

Entered by: RC Publishing Company, Inc.
National Award: **BRONZE**
Class: Wall
Division: Retail
Designer: Leon Bodzioch,
 Bodzioch Design
Photographer: Sharon White,
 White-Packard
Printer: Wintor-Swan Associates Inc.

WOLFGANG AMADEUS MOZART *Meiner Liebsten schöne Wangen*

KNP LEYKAM

Pictorial Compositions

Entered by: KNP LEYKAM Austria
Aktiengesellschaft
World Award: BRONZE
Class: Wall
Designer & Art Director: Cordula Alessandri-
Ebner
Concept & Photographer: Claudio Alessandri
Printer: Agens-Werk Geyer & Reisser

3-D Sensations Sports
Entered by: Hallmark Cards, Inc.
National Award: SILVER
Class: Wall
Division: Retail
Designer: Calendar Design Group
Printer: Commerical Lithographers
Client: Hallmark Cards, Inc.

So Far, 1995
Entered by: Mahaney & Meyers
National Award: BRONZE
Class: Miscellaneous
Division: Custom/Corporate

ADDITIONAL AWARD:
World BRONZE—Most Original

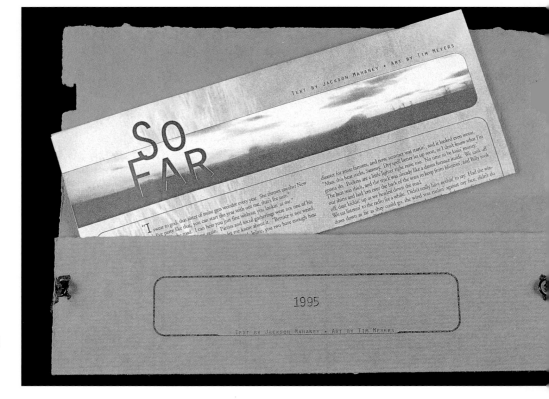

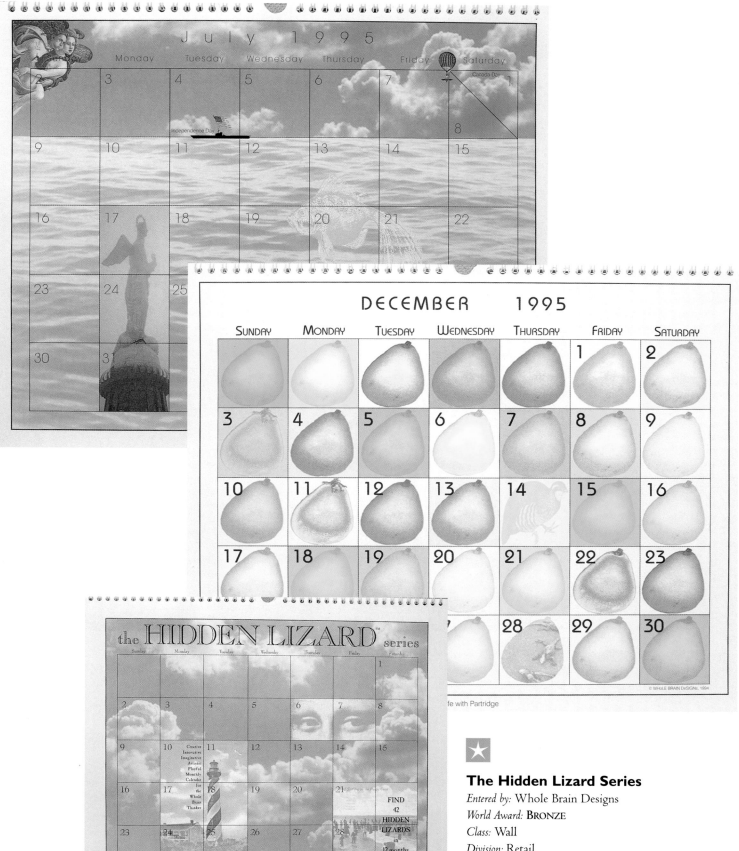

© WHOLE BRAIN DeSiGNs, 1994

...fe with Partridge

The Hidden Lizard Series

Entered by: Whole Brain Designs
World Award: **BRONZE**
Class: Wall
Division: Retail
Designers & Art Directors: Stacy Karzen
  and Carol Austin

ADDITIONAL AWARD:
National MERIT—Most Original

Words & Pictures

Entered by: Hellman Associates, Inc.
National Award: SILVER
Class: Wall
Division: Custom/Corporate
Concept: Greg Hargreaves
Designers: Ed Flack and
 Greg Hargreaves
Printer: Garner Printing

"Page of a Diary"
Autumn 1922

Entered by: John Latka & Co., Inc.,
Creative Printers

National Award: BRONZE

Class: Poster

Division: Custom/Corporate

Designer: John Latka & Co., Inc.,
Creative Printers

Photo by Allan T. Stevens taken at "Pension Bailey–Banas"

Jim Lenain *(firefighter)* Amy Koryko *(rescued boarder)* Dan Bailey *("fire chief")* Paul Banas *(firefighter)* Patricia Banas *(damsel in distress)* Lynn Herman *(Help! Help!)* Maureen Koryko *(Help! Help!)* Ron Stenkiewicz *(firefighter with ax)* Bruce Raymond *(injured professor)* Brad Banas *(assisting victim)* Joe Banas *(traveling salesman)* Murielle Falardeau Banas *(opener teacher, the nosy hunter)*

1995

JANUARY								FEBRUARY								MARCH								APRIL						
Sun	Mon	Tue	Wed	Thur	Fri	Sat		Sun	Mon	Tue	Wed	Thur	Fri	Sat		Sun	Mon	Tue	Wed	Thur	Fri	Sat		Sun	Mon	Tue	Wed	Thur	Fri	Sat
1	2	3	4	5	6	7					1	2	3	4					1	2	3	4								1
8	9	10	11	12	13	14		5	6	7	8	9	10	11		5	6	7	8	9	10	11		2	3	4	5	6	7	8
15	16	17	18	19	20	21		12	13	14	15	16	17	18		12	13	14	15	16	17	18		9	10	11	12	13	14	15
22	23	24	25	26	27	28		19	20	21	22	23	24	25		19	20	21	22	23	24	25		16	17	18	19	20	21	22
29	30	31						26	27	28						26	27	28	29	30	31			23	24	25	26	27	28	29
																								30						

MAY								JUNE								JULY								AUGUST						
Sun	Mon	Tue	Wed	Thur	Fri	Sat		Sun	Mon	Tue	Wed	Thur	Fri	Sat		Sun	Mon	Tue	Wed	Thur	Fri	Sat		Sun	Mon	Tue	Wed	Thur	Fri	Sat
	1	2	3	4	5	6						1	2	3								1				1	2	3	4	5
7	8	9	10	11	12	13		4	5	6	7	8	9	10		2	3	4	5	6	7	8		6	7	8	9	10	11	12
14	15	16	17	18	19	20		11	12	13	14	15	16	17		9	10	11	12	13	14	15		13	14	15	16	17	18	19
21	22	23	24	25	26	27		18	19	20	21	22	23	24		16	17	18	19	20	21	22		20	21	22	23	24	25	26
28	29	30	31					25	26	27	28	29	30			23	24	25	26	27	28	29		27	28	29	30	31		
																30	31													

SEPTEMBER								OCTOBER								NOVEMBER								DECEMBER						
Sun	Mon	Tue	Wed	Thur	Fri	Sat		Sun	Mon	Tue	Wed	Thur	Fri	Sat		Sun	Mon	Tue	Wed	Thur	Fri	Sat		Sun	Mon	Tue	Wed	Thur	Fri	Sat
					1	2		1	2	3	4	5	6	7					1	2	3	4							1	2
3	4	5	6	7	8	9		8	9	10	11	12	13	14		5	6	7	8	9	10	11		3	4	5	6	7	8	9
10	11	12	13	14	15	16		15	16	17	18	19	20	21		12	13	14	15	16	17	18		10	11	12	13	14	15	16
17	18	19	20	21	22	23		22	23	24	25	26	27	28		19	20	21	22	23	24	25		17	18	19	20	21	22	23
24	25	26	27	28	29	30		29	30	31						26	27	28	29	30				24	25	26	27	28	29	30
																								31						

=== DAYS TO REMEMBER • 1995 ===

New Year's Day .... January 1st	Daylight Saving Time Begins .... April 2nd	Flag Day .... June 14th	Columbus Day *(observed)* .... October 9th
Martin Luther King Day .... January 16th	Palm Sunday .... April 9th	Father's Day .... June 18th	Thanksgiving Day *(Canada)* .... October 9th
Groundhog Day .... February 2nd	Good Friday .... April 14th	Summer Begins .... June 21st	Daylight Saving Time Ends .... October 29th
Lincoln's Birthday .... February 12th	First Day of Passover .... April 15th	Canada Day *(Canada)* .... July 1st	Halloween .... October 31st
St. Valentine's Day .... February 14th	Easter Sunday .... April 16th	Independence Day .... July 4th	Veteran's Day .... November 11th
Washington's Birthday *(observed)* ... February 20th	Patriot's Day *(MA, ME)* .... April 17th	Labor Day .... September 4th	Thanksgiving Day .... November 23rd
Ash Wednesday .... March 1st	Secretaries Day .... April 26th	Autumn Begins .... September 23rd	First Day of Hanukkah .... December 18th
St. Patrick's Day .... March 17th	Mother's Day .... May 14th	First Day of Rosh Hashanah ... September 25th	Winter Begins .... December 22nd
Spring Begins .... March 20th	Memorial Day *(observed)* .... May 29th	Yom Kippur .... October 4th	Christmas Day .... December 25th

JOHN LATKA & CO., INC., PRINTING

Westfield, Massachusetts

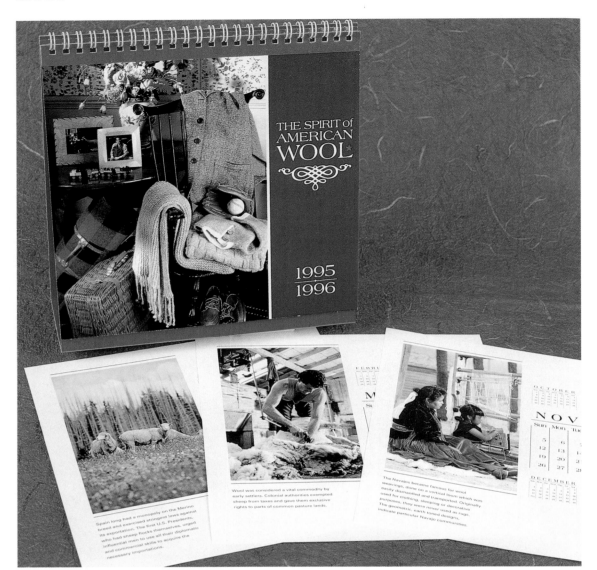

The Spirit of American Wool Calendar/ American Wool Council

Entered by: Jinno International Group and
Adrienne Youngstein & Associates
World Award: BRONZE
Class: Desk
Division: Custom/Corporate
Designer/Art Director: Adrienne Youngstein
Creative Director: Rick Wertheimer
Printer: Eurasia Press
Printing Director: Yoh Jinno
Color Separator: Pioneer Graphic Scanning

ADDITIONAL AWARDS:
World MERIT—Best Theme
National MERIT—Most Creative
Marketing Application

Lens and Light

Entered by: The Christian Science Monitor

National Award: **MERIT**

Class: Wall

Division: Custom/Corporate

Metropolitan Diary 1995

Entered by: Per Annum Inc.

National Award: **MERIT**

Class: Pocket/Planner

Division: Custom/Corporate

Best Films on Video

Entered by: Best Video

National Award: **MERIT**

Class: Wall

Division: Retail

Designer: Christopher Fenger,
 Fenger Design

7

BEST
Theme

GOLD   SILVER   BRONZE   MERIT

January

1
8
15
22
29

Vaca Key, Florida

February

Sunday	Monday	Tuesday	Wednesday	Thursday	Friday	Saturday
·	·	·	1	2	3	4
5	6	7	8	9	10	11
12	13	14	15	16	17	18
19	20	21	22	23	24	25
26	27	28	·	·	·	·

Canon

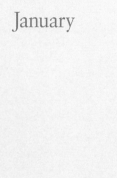

1995 Canon Calendar

Entered by: S Plus, Inc.
National Award: GOLD
Class: Wall
Division: Custom/Corporate
Designer: Kaz Akiyama, S Plus, Inc.
Art Director: Shige Shimada
Photographer: Robin Hood
Client: Canon U.S.A., Inc

PHOTOMONTAGES BY SCOTT MUTTER

SURRATIONAL IMAGES

1995 CALENDAR

PHOTOMONTAGES & TEXT © 1994 SCOTT MUTTER

April

A culture and what it produces is made possible by and is reflective of the knowledge that underlies it.

Surrational Images— Scott Mutter

Entered by: Portal Publications
National Award: GOLD
Class: Wall
Division: Retail
Designer: Sandra Belda
Art Director: Rebecca Hubert

ADDITIONAL AWARD:
 National GOLD—Most Original

National Geographic 1995 Appointment Book

Entered by:
National Geographic Society

National Award: **GOLD**

Class: Desk

Division: Retail

ADDITIONAL AWARD:

World BRONZE—Best Theme

1995 Interstate Batteries Great American Race Calendar

Entered by: Interstate Batteries

National Award: **GOLD**

Class: Wall

Division: Advertising Specialty

ADDITIONAL AWARDS:

World MERIT—Best Theme

National SILVER—Best Graphic Design, Most Original

![sunburst icon]

**365 Days in France
Calendar for 1995**

Entered by: Workman Publishing Company

World Award: GOLD

Class: Wall

Photographer: Steven Rothfeld

Text: Patricia Wells

Stretch Your Im

We go to great lengths to produce t

The possibilities are endless
when working with
Grove's extensive capabilities.

Design • Illustration

	S	M	T	W	T	F	S
JANUARY		1	2	3	4	5	6	7
	8	9	10	11	12	13	14
	15	16	17	18	19	20	21
	22	23	24	25	26	27	28
	29	30	31				

	S	M	T	W	T	F	S
FEBRUARY				1	2	3	4
	5	6	7	8	9	10	11
	12	13	14	15	16	17	18
	19	20	21	22	23	24	25
	26	27	28				

	S	M	T	W	T	F	S
MARCH				1	2	3	4
	5	6	7	8	9	10	11
	12	13	14	15	16	17	18
	19	20	21	22	23	24	25
	26	27	28	29	30	31	

Wedding Planner

Entered by: Sun Graphix USA
National Award: **SILVER**
Class: Pocket/Planner
Division: Retail
Designer & Printer: Sun Graphix USA

Stretch Your Imagination

Entered by: Grove Design & Advertising
World Award: GOLD
Class: Poster
Division: Custom/Corporate

ADDITIONAL AWARD:
National GOLD—Best Theme

The Art of Healing Children

Entered by: Napa State Hospital
 Children's Art Program
World Award: SILVER
Class: Desk
Division: Retail
Designer: Resa Shore
Photographers: Greta and Lloyd Hryciw
Project Coordinator: Al Friedman

ADDITIONAL AWARD:
National BRONZE—Best Nonprofit

Be An Electrical Safety Detective

Entered by: Pennsylvania Power & Light Company

World Award: SILVER

Class: Poster

Division: Custom/Corporate

Designer: Sharon K. Merkel

Printer: Oakes Printing Company

ADDITIONAL AWARD:

National SILVER—Best Theme

'95 Ron Schara Minnesota Sportsman's Calendar

Entered by: Wild Ideas, Inc.

National Award: SILVER

Class: Wall

Division: Advertising Specialty

ADDITIONAL AWARDS:

National BRONZE—Most Original

National MERIT—Best Graphic
 Design, Most Educational

Ultimate Sailing Calendar

Entered by: Windward
 Productions, Inc.

National Award: SILVER

Class: Wall

Division: Retail

American Panorama

Entered by: Ric Ergenbright
Photography

National Award: SILVER

Class: Desk

Division: Retail

**The Keepers
of the Culture**

Entered by: Image Design, Inc.

National Award: SILVER

Class: Desk

Division: Custom/Corporate

ADDITIONAL AWARD:

World GOLD—Best Theme

Wizard of Oz
Entered by: Hallmark Cards, Inc.
National Award: **BRONZE**
Class: Wall
Division: Retail
Designer: Calendar Design Group
Printer: Commerical Lithographers
Client: Hallmark Cards, Inc.

The 1995 Left-Hander's Desk Calendar
Entered by: Price Stern Sloan, Inc.
National Award: **BRONZE**
Class: Desk
Division: Retail

The 1995 Cycling Calendar

Entered by: Famous Cycling
  Productions
World Award: BRONZE
Class: Wall
Designer: Judy-Allen Storey
Photographer: Graham Watson
Printer: The Press, Inc.

Salvador Dali Museum 1995 Diary

Entered by: Kensington House
  Publishing Ltd.
National Award: BRONZE
Class: Desk
Division: Custom/Corporate

1995 Michigan Facts & Trivia Calendar

Entered by: Mich-Cal
National Award: MERIT
Class: Desk
Division: Retail
Art Director: James Harlan
Printer: Banta Company
Publisher: Bill Brown

Diner Time

Entered by: Luyk Miller Pelton
 Advertising
National Award: BRONZE
Class: Wall
Division: Custom/Corporate

Please Save The Animals

Entered by: Landmark General Corp.
National Award: MERIT
Class: Wall
Division: Retail

Children's Hour

Entered by: Portal Publications
National Award: MERIT
Class: Wall
Division: Retail
Designer: Sandra Belda
Art Director: Rebecca Hubert

The Art of Global Communications

Entered by: Grafica, Inc.
National Award: MERIT
Class: Wall
Division: Custom/Corporate
Designer: Rita Rovazzi
Printer: Sandy Alexander

Steam Boatin'

Entered by: New Orleans Gumbo
 Publishing
National Award: MERIT
Class: Wall
Division: Custom/Corporate

8

BEST *Cartoon Art* & MOST *Humorous*

GOLD SILVER BRONZE MERIT

Rush hour, on the New Guernsey turnpike.

©1994 Kevin Pope

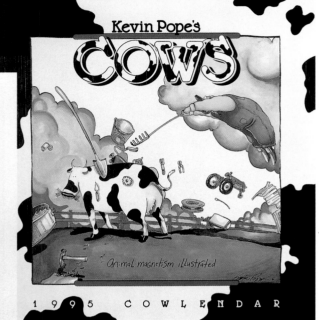

may

sunday	monday	tuesday	wednesday	thursday	friday	saturday
	1	2	3	4	5	6
7	8	9	10	11	12	13
14	15	16	17	18	19	20
21	22	23	24	25	26	27
28	29	30	31			

Kevin Pope's Cows

Entered by: Portal Publications
National Award: GOLD
Class: Wall
Division: Retail
Designer & Art Director: Jennifer Reno

CARTOON ART

Ballard Street

Entered by: Day Dream Publishing, Inc.

National Award: SILVER

Class: Wall

Division: Retail

Printer: Shepard Poorman
  Communications Corporation

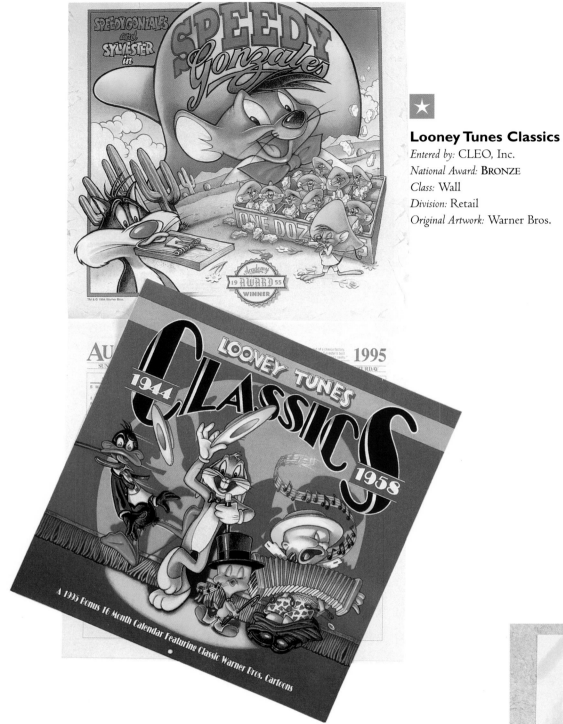

★ **Looney Tunes Classics**

Entered by: CLEO, Inc.

National Award: **BRONZE**

Class: Wall

Division: Retail

Original Artwork: Warner Bros.

The Busy Woman Calendar with Tips for Coping Through 1995

Entered by: Current, Inc.

National Award: **MERIT**

Class: Wall

Division: Retail

🌟

Saturday Night Live
Entered by: Hallmark Cards, Inc.
National Award: GOLD
Class: Wall
Division: Retail
Designer: Calendar Design Group
Printer: Commercial Lithographers
Client: Hallmark Cards, Inc.

MOST HUMOROUS

The 365 Stupidest Things Ever Said Page-A-Day® Calendar by Ross and Kathryn Petras
Entered by: Workman Publishing Company
National Award: SILVER
Class: Desk
Division: Retail

1995 Cowlendar
Entered by: Reiman Publications
National Award: SILVER
Class: Wall
Division: Retail

Bob & Tom's History of the World

Entered by: WFBQ Radio
National Award: SILVER
Class: Wall
Division: Custom/Corporate
Artist: John Childress
Printer: Shepard Poorman
  Communications Corporation
Project Coordinator: Pam Ferrin

1995 Pig Calendar

Entered by: Reiman Publications
National Award: BRONZE
Class: Wall
Division: Retail

It's a Dog's Life: A 1995 Calendar

Entered by: Current, Inc.
National Award: BRONZE
Class: Wall
Division: Retail

Clyde & Sadie

Entered by: JII/Sales Promotion
  Associates, Inc.
National Award: **BRONZE**
Class: Wall
Division: Advertising Specialty
Artist: Darrel Rhubee
Designer & Printer: JII/Sales
  Promotion Associates, Inc.

Culver Calendar

Entered by: Culver Design
National Award: **BRONZE**
Class: Poster
Division: Custom/Corporate

9

BEST *Children's* & MOST *Educational*

GOLD   SILVER   BRONZE   MERIT

CHILDREN'S

The 1995 Lisbeth Zwerger Calendar

Entered by: North-South Books

National Award: GOLD

Class: Wall

Division: Retail

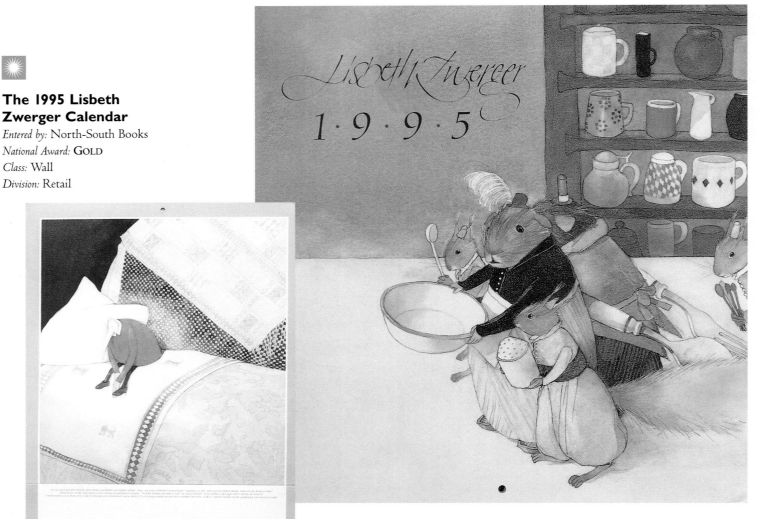

AGNÈS MATHIEU

AUGUST

SUNDAY	MONDAY	TUESDAY	WEDNESDAY	THURSDAY	FRIDAY	SATURDAY
		1	2	3	4	5
6	7	8	9	10	11	12
13	14	15	16	17	18	19
20	21	22	23	24	25	26
27	28	29	30	31		

The 1995 Magical Menagerie Calendar
Entered by: North-South Books
National Award: SILVER
Class: Wall
Division: Retail

★

The Lion King

Entered by: Day Dream
 Publishing, Inc.
National Award: **BRONZE**
Class: Wall
Division: Retail
Printer: Shepard Poorman
 Communications
 Corporation

ADDITIONAL AWARD:
World MERIT—
 Best Graphic Design

★

**1995 Safety Art Contest
Calendar**

Entered by: Communication Design, Inc.
National Award: Bronze
Class: Wall
Division: Custom/Corporate
Designers: Bill Cullen,
 Robert Meganck, and Tim Priddy
Client: Virginia Power

Bessie Pease Gutmann
Entered by: Portal Publications
National Award: MERIT
Class: Wall
Division: Retail
Designer: Raul Del Rio
Art Director: Jennifer Reno

Wildlife Alert!
Entered by: National
 Geographic Society
National Award: MERIT
Class: Wall
Division: Retail

EDUCATIONAL

The Money Chronicle

Entered by: Lakeside Marketing
 Services, Inc.

National Award: **GOLD**

Class: Wall

Division: Advertising Specialty

Designer: Leo Zayauskas-Design, Inc.

Photographer: Nawrocki Stock Photo, Inc.

Printer: Darwill Press

ADDITIONAL AWARD:
National SILVER—Most Original

Great Gardens

Entered by: Portal Publications
National Award: **GOLD**
Class: Wall
Divison: Retail
Designer: Sandra Belda
Art Director: Jennifer Reno

Saving our Children & Youth

Entered by: T.P. Design, Inc.
National Award: **GOLD**
Class: Wall
Division: Custom/Corporate
Designer: T.P. Design, Inc.
Cover Illustrator: Charly Palmer
Photographer: EW Productions, Inc.

365 Matters of Fact: The Encyclopedia Britannica Page-A-Day® Calendar

Entered by: Workman Publishing
  Company
National Award: SILVER
Class: Desk
Division: Retail

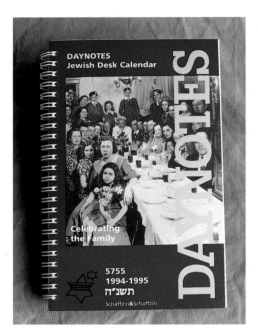

Daynotes Jewish
Desk Calendar

Entered by: Schaffzin & Schaffzin
National Award: SILVER
Class: Desk
Division: Custom/Corporate
Designer: Stephen Schaffzin
Printer: Automated Graphic Systems
Researcher: Linda K. Schaffzin

People and Animals:
United For Health

Entered by: The Burlington Group
National Award: SILVER
Class: Poster
Division: Custom/Corporate
Designer & Illustrator:
  Lynne Beighley Abell
Printer: Acme Printing
Curriculum Development: Leslie Nader, Ph.D.

ADDITIONAL AWARD:
  National SILVER—Best Children's

Senate of Pennsylvania 1995

Entered by: Senate of PA,
  Republican Communications

National Award: SILVER

Class: Wall

Division: Custom/Corporate

Designer: Deborah Marks

Photographer: Brian Foster

Prepress: Fidelity Color, Inc.

Printer: Sowers Printing

1995 FHP, Inc. Senior Plan Health Calendar

Entered by: American Custom
  Publishing, Inc.

National Award: SILVER

Class: Wall

Division: Advertising Specialty

Art Director: Patricia Henze

1995 Alaska Weather Calendar

Entered by: Williwaw Publishing Co.
National Award: SILVER
Class: Wall
Division: Retail
Designer & Editor: Jim Green
Printer: Northern Printing

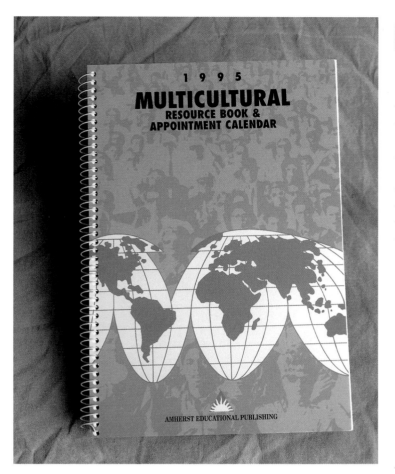

1995 Multicultural Resource Book & Appointment Calendar

Entered by: Amherst Educational Publishing
National Award: BRONZE
Class: Pocket/Planner
Division: Retail
Designer: Pioneer Training
Editor: Kristin O'Connell
Printer: The Paper House

Sonoran Desert

Entered by: Environmental Arts Center
National Award: SILVER
Class: Poster
Division: Custom/Corporate
Designers & Illustrators: Virge Kask and Bev Benner
Printer: Precision Offset Printing Co.

★

1995 Backyard Gardener Calendar

Entered by: University of Connecticut
National Award: **BRONZE**
Class: Wall
Division: Custom/Corporate
Designer: Karen J. Yurgilevich-Havens
Editor: Carl A. Salsedo
Printer: Thames Printing Co.

〰

Venice Beach 1995 Historical Calendar

Entered by: Constitutional Capers
National Award: **MERIT**
Class: Wall
Division: Retail
Designer: Lionel Banks

10

M O S T

Creative Marketing Application

GOLD SILVER BRONZE MERIT

PERHAPS THE FIRST AND GREATEST OF MAN'S DISCOVERIES WAS TIME. AND ALONG WITH THAT CAME THE ABILITY TO PREDICT THE SEASONS. THE ONSET OF SPRING. THE COMING OF RAIN. THE PLANTING OF CROPS. BY THE MARKING OF DAYS, MANKIND WAS LIBERATED FROM THE CYCLICAL MONOTONY OF NATURE AND COULD MEANINGFULLY MEASURE HIS MOVEMENT ACROSS THE PLANET.

Day Dream Corporate Credential Piece

Entered by: Day Dream
    Publishing, Inc.
National Award: GOLD
Class: Miscellaneous
Division: Custom/Corporate
Printer: Shepard Poorman
    Communications Corporation

Waterloo Industries Automotive Calendar
Entered by: Hellman Associates, Inc.
National Award: GOLD
Class: Poster
Division: Custom/Corporate
Art Director: David McNurlen
Printer: Garner Printing

Republic's Employee-Owners Behind the Scenes

Entered by: Innis Maggiore Group
National Award: **GOLD**
Class: Wall
Division: Custom/Corporate

ADDITIONAL AWARDS:

World SILVER—Best Theme
National SILVER—Best Graphic
  Design, Best Theme

Springhill Desk Calendar

Entered by: Oden & Associates
National Award: **GOLD**
Class: Desk
Division: Custom/Corporate
Designer: Bill Berry
Illustrator: Daphne Hewitt
Printer: Sigma Marketing

ADDITIONAL AWARD:

World SILVER—Best Use of Paper

**Texins Credit Union
1995 Planning Calendar**

Entered by: The Summit Group
National Award: **SILVER**
Class: Miscellaneous
Division: Custom/Corporate

Cool Crew 1995

Entered by: Igloo Products Corp.
National Award: **SILVER**
Class: Poster
Division: Custom/Corporate
Designer: Applewhite/Adams Design
Photographers: Andis Applewhite
  and Stephen Hamilton
Printer: Jolley Printing, Inc.

B O L G E R 1 9 9 5

1910 Farm family near Underwood.

Photograph by Carl Evenson/Minnesota Historical Society

1 Sunday		16 Monday	
2 Monday		17 Tuesday	
3 Tuesday		18 Wednesday	
4 Wednesday	Yom Kippur	19 Thursday	
5 Thursday		20 Friday	
6 Friday		21 Saturday	
7 Saturday		22 Sunday	
8 Sunday		23 Monday	
9 Monday	Columbus Day	24 Tuesday	
10 Tuesday		25 Wednesday	
11 Wednesday		26 Thursday	
12 Thursday		27 Friday	
13 Friday		28 Saturday	
14 Saturday		29 Sunday	
15 Sunday		30 Monday	
		31 Tuesday	Halloween

o c t o b e r

Minnesota Remembered

Entered by: Bolger Publications/
Creative Printing
National Award: **SILVER**
Class: Desk
Divisions: Custom/Corporate,
Technical
Designer: Michael Vogt
Color Separator & Printer:
Bolger Publications/Creative
Printing

ADDITIONAL AWARDS:
World BRONZE—Best Theme
National SILVER—Best Use of Paper

We Fit Your Life Perfectly

Entered by: W. T. Quinn Advertising & Marketing
National Award: SILVER
Class: Desk
Division: Retail
Designer: Wendy Sugarman

Glendale Galleria—
A Special Spirit

Entered by: The Royle Communications Group
National Award: SILVER
Class: Wall
Division: Custom/Corporate
Creative Director: Terry Jenkins
Photographer: Kelly Sims
Printer: The Royle Communications Group
Color Separator: American Color
Client: Mall Design Advertising

1995 Miller Lite Ice

Entered by: Gib Black Advertising Group
National Award: SILVER
Class: Poster
Division: Retail
Designer: Jackie Black
Photographer: Tom Servais
Printer: General Printing

The 1995 Book Lover's Page-A-Day® Calendar

Entered by: Workman Publishing
  Company
National Award: SILVER
Class: Desk
Division: Technical

Rope

Entered by: Barbara Brown
  Marketing & Design
National Award: **BRONZE**
Class: Poster
Division: Custom/Corporate
Printer: Ventura Printing

ADDITIONAL AWARDS:
National BRONZE—Best Theme
National MERIT—Best Graphic Design

A Pictorial Tour of Graphics Universal Incorporated

Entered by: Graphics Universal
  Incorporated
National Award: **BRONZE**
Class: Miscellaneous
Division: Custom/Corporate
Designers: Terry Cain and
  Ralph DeVore
Printer & Color Separator: Graphics
  Universal Incorporated

ADDITIONAL AWARD:
World SILVER—Most Original

1995 Hooters Calendar

Entered by: Provident Advertising
  and Marketing
National Award: **BRONZE**
Class: Wall
Division: Retail

Visalia Press 1995 Calendar

Entered by: Visalia Press & Printing Center Incorporated

National Award: BRONZE

Class: Desk

Division: Custom/Corporate

Designer: Vaneno-Warren Inc.

Kroger HEALTHhints 1995 Calendar

Entered by: Seltzer, Kaufmann & McGraw, Inc.

National Award: BRONZE

Class: Wall

Division: Advertising Specialty

Designer & Art Director: Jeanne Trahey

Illustrator: Robert Tanenbaum

DuPont Top Gun

Entered by: Calendar Promotions
National Award: MERIT
Class: Wall
Divisions: Custom/Corporate, Technical

ADDITIONAL AWARD:
National MERIT—Best Printing

1995 Colonial Penn Calendar

Entered by: American Custom Publishing, Inc.
National Award: MERIT
Class: Wall
Divisions: Advertising Specialty
Art Director: Patricia Henze

The Choice is Crystal Clear.

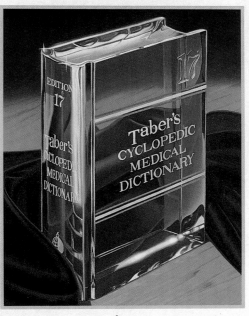

Taber's
Always up to date!

1995

F.A. Davis: Taber's Calendar
Entered by: Kingswood Advertising, Inc.
National Award: MERIT
Class: Poster
Division: Custom/Corporate
Designer: Stephanie Dais
Illustrator: Randy Hamlin
Art Director: Mary Senkarik
Creative Director: Ed Dahl
Printer & Color Separator: Colorlith

1995 Theme Pleaser
Entered by: Gardner Merchant
Food Services
National Award: MERIT
Class: Wall
Division: Custom/Corporate
Designer: Gardner Merchant
Graphics Department
Printer: Unigraphic Printing

A Colorful Affair
Entered by: Jersey Printing
Associates, Inc.
National Award: MERIT
Class: Poster
Division: Custom/Corporate
Designer: Jersey Printing
Associates, Inc.
Photographer: Frank Peluso
Photography
Color Separator: Eagle Graphics, Inc.

Lake Erie Graphics, 1995
Entered by: Ramba Design
National Award: MERIT
Class: Desk
Division: Custom/Corporate
Designers: Kerry Prugh and Brian Sooy
Printer: Lake Erie Graphics, Inc.

11

BEST
Nonprofit

GOLD   SILVER   BRONZE   MERIT

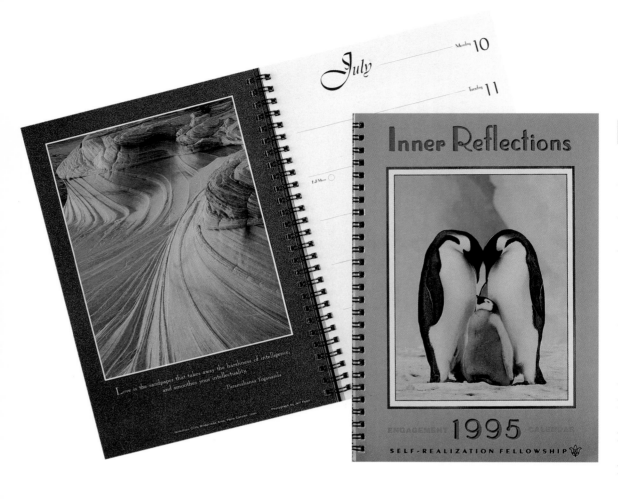

Inner Reflections
Entered by: Self-Realization
  Fellowship
National Award: **GOLD**
Class: Desk
Divisions: Retail, Technical
Printer: Tien Wah Press,
  Strategy Advertising
Color Separator: Color Service

ADDITIONAL AWARDS:
World SILVER—Best Printing,
  Best Nature/Scenic Photography,
  Best Color Separation
World MERIT—Best Graphic Design
National SILVER—Best Color
  Separation, Best Printing
National BRONZE—Best Theme,
  Best Graphic Design
National MERIT—Best Nature/
  Scenic Photography

Utah 1995
Entered by: Utah Travel Council
National Award: **GOLD**
Class: Wall
Division: Custom/Corporate
Designer: Scott Hardy Design
Printer: American Graphics
Publications Director: Janice Carpenter

ADDITIONAL AWARDS:
World MERIT—Best Graphic
  Design, Best Nature/Scenic
  Photography

THE CATSKILLS

1995 CALENDAR

PUBLISHED BY THE CATSKILL CENTER FOR CONSERVATION AND DEVELOPMENT, INC.

NOVEMBER

SUNDAY	MONDAY	TUESDAY	WEDNESDAY	THURSDAY	FRIDAY	SATURDAY
			1	2	3	4
5	6	7	8	9	10	11
12	13	14	15	16	17	18
19	20	21	22	23	24	25
26	27	28	29	30		

The Catskills

Entered by: The Catskill Center
National Award: GOLD
Class: Wall
Division: Retail
Designer: Jerry Novesky
Photographers: Tom Teich, Hardie
 Truesdale, Simon Russell, and
 Robert Hansen-Sturm
Printer: Regal Art Press

WWF Wildlife
of the World

Entered by: Day Dream
 Publishing, Inc.
National Award: GOLD
Class: Wall
Division: Retail
Printer: Shepard Poorman
 Communications Corporation

Phragmipedium besseae

AUGUST

SUNDAY	MONDAY	TUESDAY	WEDNESDAY	THURSDAY	FRIDAY	SATURDAY
		1	2	3	4	5
6	7	8	9	10	11	12
13	14	15	16	17	18	19
20	21	22	23	24	25	26
27	28	29	30	31		

**The Nature Conservancy
1995 Wall Calendar**

Entered by: Falcon Press Publishing

National Award: **GOLD**

Class: Wall

Division: Retail

1995 Corporate American Wildlife Calendar

Entered by: Union Camp Corporation

National Award: **GOLD**

Class: Wall

Division: Custom/Corporate

Concept, Text, & Illustration: Robert S. Todd

Printer: Graphic Management, Inc.

The Nature Conservancy 1995 Desk Calendar

Entered by: Falcon Press Publishing

National Award: **SILVER**

Class: Desk

Division: Retail

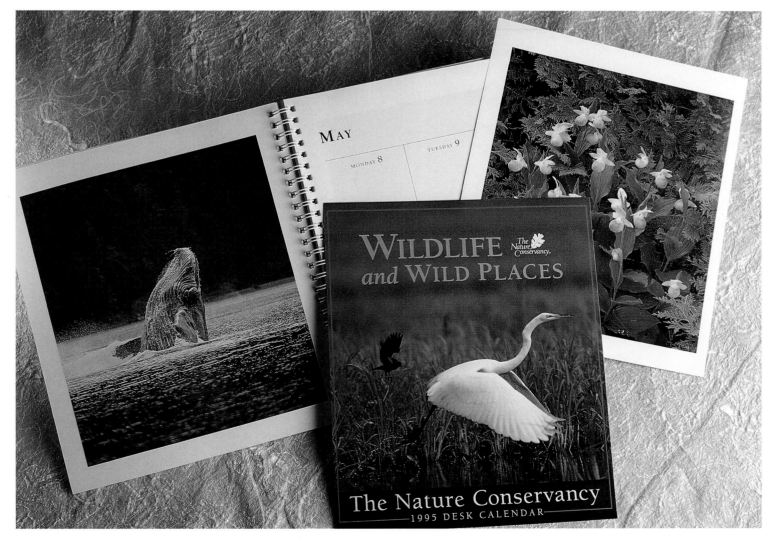

Greyhound Friends
1995 Calendar

Entered by: Greyhound Friends, Inc.
National Award: SILVER
Class: Wall
Division: Custom/Corporate
Designer: Denise McFadden
Hand Colorist: Gabrielle Mottern
Photographer: John Mottern
Printer: Mount Auburn Press

1995 Corporate Calendar

Entered by: Bush Roake Allen, Inc.
National Award: SILVER
Class: Poster
Division: Custom/Corporate
Electronic Imaging: BC Communications
Concept & Art Director: Robert S. Todd
Printer: Sandy Alexander, Inc.

Un-Stress Calendar

Entered by: Lakeview Center, Inc.

National Award: SILVER

Class: Miscellaneous

Division: Custom/Corporate

Artist: Chris Carr

Team Members: Peggy Mika and
 Becky Siegel

Printer: Boyd Brothers, Inc.

Text: Linda Roush

ADDITIONAL AWARD:
National SILVER—Best Theme

Art Auction Calendar

Entered by: Wenz-Neely
National Award: SILVER
Class: Wall
Division: Custom/Corporate
Designer: Leslie Friesen
Printer: Merrick Printing

Adirondack Mountain Club 1995 Calendar

Entered by: Adirondack
  Mountain Club
National Award: BRONZE
Class: Wall
Division: Retail
Designer: Marjolaine Arsenault,
  Idee Design
Printer: Excelsior Printing

1995 Federal Disaster Calendar

Entered by: Competitive Enterprise
  Institute
National Award: BRONZE
Class: Wall
Division: Custom/Corporate
Designers: Sam Kazman and
  Alexander Volokh

Dishes

Entered by: CLEO, Inc.
National Award: BRONZE
Class: Wall
Division: Retail
Designer: Glen Marshall,
  CLEO, Inc.

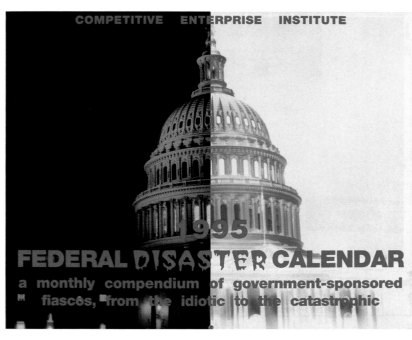

Lift Up Your Hearts

Entered by: Trinity Missions
National Award: BRONZE
Class: Pocket/Planner
Division: Custom/Corporate

ADDITIONAL AWARD:
World MERIT—
   Best Contemporary Art

We Change the World One Girl at a Time

Entered by: San Francisco Bay Girl
   Scout Council
National Award: BRONZE
Class: Pocket/Planner
Division: Custom/Corporate
Designer: Barbara Lande
Photographer: Billy Hustace
Printer: Shepard Poorman
   Communications Corporation
Project Coordinator: Anita "Kit"
   Thompson
Text: Jack Soares